Unquenchable Determination

The Joys and Challenges of Mission Work

"I will never leave you, nor forsake you."
Hebrews 13:5

Ruth V. Sammons, Ed. D. Miss.

Copyright© 2017 Ruth V. Sammons, Ed. D. Miss.
All rights reserved

Cover layout by Stephen Sammons, D. Min.

ISBN 13: 978-1542733861
ISBH 10: 1542733863

CONTENTS

	Page
Preface	v
Introduction—Challenged for Missions	1
Chapter 1 — Missionary Training and Marriage	7
Chapter 2 — Asunción, Paraguay, 1962	11
Chapter 3 — Lima Ty	19
Chapter 4 — Move to Tupãrenda	23
Chapter 5 — More Tupãrenda Experiences	33
Chapter 6 — Literacy and the Angaite Tupãrenda Church	61
Chapter 7 — Home Assignment	65
Return to Paraguay	68
Chapter 8 — 1972 Home Assignment	71
Return to Paraguay—New Assignment	73
Chapter 9 — Move to Cerro Morotĩ—Ache Village	79
Chapter 10 — Moving Again	88
Chapter 11 — Home Assignment—New Tribes Bible Institute	95
Chapter 12 — Back in Paraguay	99
Chapter 13 — Moving from the Apartment to a House	109
Chapter 14 — Back in Asunción—August 1988	113
Chapter 15 — Year 1990	122
Chapter 16 — Year 1991	126
Chapter 17 — Year 1992–May 1993	130
In Transition	134
Chapter 18 — Living in Colonia San Carlos	139
Chapter 19 — Marxist Agitation	149
Chapter 20 — Life in Concepción	153
Chapter 21 — Move to the USA	163
Lessons Learned	169
50th Anniversary	177

Though the fig tree should not blossom,
And there be no fruit on the vines,
Though the yield of the olive should fail,
And the fields produce no food,
Though the flock should be cut off from the fold,
And there be no cattle in the stalls,
Yet I will exult in the Lord,
I will rejoice in the God of my salvation.
The Lord God is my strength,
And He has made my feet like hinds' feet,
And makes me walk on my high places.
(Habakkuk 3:17–19, NASB)

PREFACE

This book presents a brief overview of our years with New Tribes Mission in Paraguay, South America. Our ministry there was from 1962-2005. We are grateful for having had the opportunity to serve the Lord on the mission field so that others might have the opportunity to hear the truth of the gospel, realize the freedom that comes from believing and accepting Jesus Christ as Savior, and experience the joy of looking forward to spending eternity with Him.

The story of our lives would likely have been very different had it not been for the fact that we had parents who loved the Lord and believed in reaching indigenous people in other countries who hadn't yet had a chance to hear the gospel. They were supportive of our choice of ministry, even though it meant our living far away where they would rarely see us or even have the opportunity to know their grandchildren.

We are grateful for Bible-believing, mission-minded churches and individuals who were faithful to pray for us and give so that we might be able to serve the Lord in a foreign country.

We thank the Lord for godly men and women who were our mentors, teachers, and leaders throughout our years of Bible School, missionary training, and years of ministry on the field. We will never forget those kindred-spirit associates with whom we worked over the years.

The indigenous people with whom we lived and worked have definitely marked our lives forever, teaching us more about ourselves than we could ever have learned had we not lived in that cross-cultural situation.

Our own kids have perhaps been our greatest teachers and encouragers. To them we say: "Thank you for your love and forgiving spirits when we didn't always *do it right*."

> "But I do not account my life of any value nor as precious to myself, if only I may finish my course and the ministry that I received from the Lord Jesus, to testify to the gospel of the grace of God." (Acts 20:24)

Ruthie Sammons
Ramona, California

"and with your blood you purchased men for God from every tribe
and language and people and nation."
(Revelation 5:9, NIV)

MY PACESETTER

The Lord is my pacesetter, I shall not rush.
He makes me to stop for quiet intervals.
He provides me with images of stillness which restore my serenity.
He leads me in ways of efficiency through calmness of mind,
and His guidance is peace.
Even though I have a great many things to accomplish each day,
I will not fret, for His presence is here.
His timelessness, His all-importance will keep me in balance.
He prepares refreshment in the midst of my activity
by anointing my mind with His oil of tranquility.
My cup of joyous energy overflows.
Surely harmony and effectiveness shall be the fruit of my hours,
And I shall walk in the pace of the Lord and dwell in His house forever.
Author unknown

INTRODUCTION
CHALLENGED FOR MISSIONS

Growing up in a Christian family and a mission-minded church, I had an interest in missions for as long as I can remember. I was saved at an evangelistic campaign in my home church at the age of six and sang my first solo, "I'll Go Where You Want Me to Go" at that age. Our home was always open to visiting missionaries, so I had the opportunity to become acquainted with many missionaries personally. When other kids talked about what they wanted to be when they grew up, I always knew I wanted to be a foreign missionary—going to where people had not yet had the opportunity to hear the truth of the gospel.

My dad worked on the railroad and had his own auto mechanic business at home. He had half ownership in a small Cessna airplane and enjoyed flying and working on planes as well. But the day came when my parents felt God was calling them to something different; they were challenged to go into missionary training. I was twelve years old at the time and thrilled that my parents were interested in going to the mission field. It looked like God was answering my heart's desire sooner than expected.

My dad gathered up his mechanic's tools, and we pulled them in a trailer behind us, as we—my parents and we six kids—traveled from North Platte, Nebraska, to a missionary training center of New Tribes Mission, located at Fouts Springs in northern California. My parents went to classes in the mornings, and my dad was on work detail in the afternoons, working in the mechanic shop—sometimes on cars and sometimes on the mission leader's small airplane.

This was missionary "boot camp" training, so the cabins had no electricity or running water. There was a public washhouse with showers and wringer washers, available for doing laundry. Our refrigerator was an apple crate covered with straw and a gunnysack—on which a bucket of water was poured to help keep it cool—attached to the outside of the cabin.

There were times when my parents had no money, but I never ever heard them complain. When they didn't have money for groceries, they prayed, and God provided in amazing ways. We kids never worried about it—we never went without a meal. There was always *something* to eat.

We weren't fussy eaters and never complained about the food. We learned to "eat to live," *not* "live to eat."

Upon my parents' completion of their training, my dad, being a pilot and mechanic, was asked to go to Venezuela to serve as the mission pilot. There was no flight program in Venezuela at the time. *But it was not to be.* My mom had started to pack our things to leave the training center when there was a big forest fire to which all the men in camp were called to help fight. My dad was one of the fourteen men who never returned. The fire had been lit by someone needing work—hoping he would be hired to cook for the fire fighters, never intending that anyone die. Twenty-eight missionary candidates went out on that fire; fourteen of them died, along with one forest ranger.

My dad was thirty-seven years old, and my mother was thirty-two. We were then seven children; I was thirteen years old, and the youngest was two months old. Though my mother was asked to stay and teach linguistics, at which she was proficient, she declined; and five months later we returned to Nebraska.

Sometime during that five months' time at the boot camp another crisis took place that I will never forget. My baby brother turned blue and quit breathing for no apparent reason. Medical help was a long way away. The elders were quickly called to pray for him according to the Biblical instructions of James 5; as they prayed, Bobby just relaxed in Mother's arms and was okay again. That made a strong impression on me and strengthened my personal faith in God's answering prayer.

Four of the seven of us kids ended up going to the mission field as missionaries after growing up, marrying and completing missionary training. One sister died at the age of twenty-five after surgery here in the United States while on furlough, leaving a husband and two young sons. One of the sisters-in-law died on the mission field, leaving a husband and four young children. Both remaining spouses remarried and continued in full-time ministry. Some of my nephews and nieces now serve on the mission field as well.

A year after my dad died, my mom married a widower with six children, making us a family of thirteen children. From that marriage we have a half-sister; thus, we became a family of sixteen individuals. The two families were well acquainted with each other long before the death of either spouse; we had our own choir and orchestra after the two families joined together!

Ten years later Mother was left a widow again. After the remaining children left home, she joined the Child Evangelism Fellowship. In 1973 she married a bachelor Baptist preacher, who acquired more than thirty grandkids immediately. He died in 1996 of long-standing health problems.

Mother went to be with the Lord in January 2006. She had no earthly goods to leave behind, but as one of my brothers said at her funeral, "She left us a legacy of three things: our faith, a good work ethic, and music—and that is enough." Well said.

Though not all was perfect in our big family (and whose is?), we have much for which to be grateful. God has used all that happened in our lives to help develop us into the kind of people He wanted us to be, so that we might be better prepared to serve Him.

This is a picture of twelve of us with mother at a family reunion. Paul was in Venezuela, unable to be present; Judy was with the Lord

People for whom Christ died.

One of the greatest blessings in life we as individuals enjoy is the God-given power *to choose*. We were created by God with a free will. What a great truth and privilege that is. The fact that some people abuse that right and choose wrongly doesn't negate the privilege that is ours to choose what we will say *yes* to in life and what we will say *no* to. There are, however, at least two things in life over which we have no choice. We did not choose our place of birth, nor did we choose our biological parents.

We were each created to be uniquely different from anyone else in this world—no *cookie cutter* robots. Each of us has a specific purpose for being born into this world.

What impact does my place of birth have on my life? Would not my life have been very different had I been born and raised in a country other than the United States of America—say China, India, or in a South American jungle to native parents? What effect did being born to Harold Jesse and Jennie Ethel Griffis have on my life?

Every life situation we experience—whether positive or negative—affects our lives in one way or another. Our response to each situation we encounter will make the difference as to whether we stunt our own personal growth by becoming resentful and critical or *grow* and mature through the experience, becoming stable, objective individuals. I'm convinced we can learn something from everyone. Not all relationships have been pleasant ones. Some have been downright difficult. What have we learned from those situations?

As a follower of the Lord Jesus Christ, I believe that nothing comes to me but what God has allowed. And although it is my desire to please the Lord and to walk according to His Word the best I know how, that does not mean I'm not going to face trials or relational struggles. Though I've often found it difficult to appreciate a trial at the time I was going through it, looking back later I've generally recognized God's hand at work in my life for a particular purpose, and I have been able to be thankful to Him that He knew what was best for me in the situation.

This walk of *faith* is exactly that. Either I believe God is for me, or I don't. If God is for me (which I believe He is), then I must believe that He knows what is best for me and that He is watching out for my good, knowing my heart's desire is to please Him. My idea of how my life is to bring glory to Him and His idea of how that is going to take place may not agree at all.

God knew what he was doing when He gave me the parents he did. He knew the kind of husband I needed, the kind of children I needed, the kind of co-workers I needed. Did I always appreciate the kind of relationships I was put into? Did I at times struggle, thinking that being in a different place with different people would be easier? The bottom line was: *Did I want God's will or my own?*

For my thoughts are not your thoughts, neither are your ways my ways, declares the LORD. For as the heavens are higher than the earth, so are my ways higher than your ways and my thoughts than your thoughts. (Isa. 55:8-9)

These verses became a reality to us while in training, and we have found them to be just as true in all the years following, no matter what our situation. God had promised to provide, and God always keeps His promises.

> "But seek first the kingdom of God and His righteousness;
> and all these things shall be added to you."
> *Matthew 6:33*

> "But my God shall supply all your need according to His riches
> in glory by Christ Jesus."
> *Philippians 4:19*

1
Missionary Training and Marriage

All through my high school years my focus remained on one day serving the Lord on the mission field as a cross-cultural missionary. Upon graduating from high school I entered the New Tribes Bible Institute in Milwaukee, Wisconsin, to begin preparation for missionary work.

Fred was in his last year at Moody Bible Institute in Chicago while I was finishing my studies at New Tribes Bible Institute. Fred's sister was also a student at NTBI at that time. As a pianist at the Wisconsin Tabernacle where Fred's parents attended church, and knowing Fred's sister, I had the opportunity to become acquainted with Mom and Dad Sammons, who then encouraged Fred to meet me. Fred told his dad at the time, "If I can't choose one girl from five hundred at Moody, what makes you think I'd choose one of fifteen from New Tribes?"

Fred and I officially met after a chili soup dinner at a tobogganing party hosted by his parents on New Year's Eve, 1957. By some strange coincidence, Fred and I ended up in the living room visiting. I remember making it clear that I had in mind to go to the mission field, and I wasn't about to be deterred by anything or anyone.

Fred wrote me a letter by way of his sister after returning to Moody. Thus began a steady correspondence between us; we saw each other when he was home for holiday weekends. We were engaged in June 1958, after both of us had graduated from our respective Bible Institutes and were married on September 27, 1958, in my home church in Nebraska.

We lived that first month with Fred's parents in Muskego, Wisconsin. We entered missionary training with New Tribes Mission in Jersey Shore, Pennsylvania, in October 1958, along with Fred's sister Dawn. When Fred's pastor in Wisconsin heard that Fred was planning to go into missionary training with New Tribes Mission, he pulled me aside and said, "This isn't going to work. Fred will *never* go along with NTM's financial policy. More than likely he will quit once he realizes what it's like." I said to the pastor, "Please do me a favor. Keep that opinion to yourself, and let Fred find out for himself."

As a "faith" mission, New Tribes Mission members were not to solicit funds, but to look to God for prayer warriors and for those who of their own accord desired to help support them in their ministries. Many people on the outside criticized that policy. (And the financial policy is somewhat different today.) But back then I had been around New Tribes Mission personnel long enough to know that being on the inside looking out was different from being on the outside looking in. Fred said, "I'm going into NTM with the idea that if the Lord can provide for us through training, He can provide for us on the field."

We never had more than ten dollars a month promised to us the whole time we were in training. Most churches at that time didn't support missionary students or candidates. They waited to see if the candidates were going to make it overseas before contributing to their support. That was true of many "home" churches—ours included.

During the first part of our time at the training institute, we lived in a *little* one-room cabin. This was missionary "boot camp," so there was no running water or bathroom in the cabin. We went to the washhouse to use the bathroom and to shower, get drinking water, get water to wash dishes, and so on. It was good preparation for the mission field.

We cooked on a two-burner white gas camp stove; for heat we had a little potbelly wood stove in which we burned coal. Before we even had orientation I did a *no–no*. We had just finished an evening meeting in the chapel and had invited a visiting mission executive committee member to have lunch with us on the following day. So I went back to the cabin alone to start working on something toward the next day's meal while Fred stayed visiting in the chapel.

The cabin was super cold, so I decided to build a fire with a bit of kindling and some coal. It refused to take off, so I decided to throw some kerosene on it from a jar outside the door, into which I had previously seen Fred put some sticks of kindling to help start a fire.

I *thought* it was kerosene. It was white gas! The gas was in a quart jar and the fire caught the jar in my hand on fire. I didn't dare drop it—I could burn down the cabin—so I threw it outside, dumping a bucket of water on it, not knowing that wasn't the thing to do, and the fire spread fast. Talk about scared! Immediately there were two men standing next to me to see if I was okay. Who should it be but the Institute director and the visiting executive committee member from the mission headquarters. Talk about embarrassing! The camp director took me to the camp nurse. I slept painfully for days! He nicknamed me "Smokey" thereafter.

We thoroughly enjoyed our boot camp days. Fred never once considered quitting. We attended classes in the morning, had work detail in the afternoons, and studied in the evenings.

One day in the classroom, as they were planning the work detail schedule, it was mentioned that the washhouse and all of the cabins at the lower end of the camp needed to be rewired; they asked if any of the students present knew how to do electrical wiring. No one raised a hand, so Fred raised his.

I said to Fred, "Do you know how to do that?" He said, "No, but I can get a book and learn." His dad had taught him that he could do anything anyone else could do, and he was willing to try anything. I was grateful for that many times on the mission field.

Fred read up on electrical wiring, and one day a master electrician from Bethlehem Steel drove into the camp. He went to see the camp director, told him who he was and what his work was, and that he wasn't sure why, but God had laid it upon his heart to stop there. The camp director took him to meet Fred.

Fred did the work; the master electrician came every week to check out his work and give helpful instructions for the following week. Eventually, the work was completed. Fred learned a lot doing that project, and he's done a lot of electrical work since.

Jungle Camp

All missionary students attended a two-week Jungle Camp sometime during their training. We were required to build our own shelter out in the woods next to a river, where we would cook, do our laundry, and so on. We weren't allowed to leave the Jungle Camp site during that two weeks. Various men were chosen to go do the grocery shopping for the rest of us; we wrote a list of the things we wanted and gave them the money with which to purchase those items. I don't remember a lot about it now, but it was an interesting experience. Though I was pregnant at the time, we didn't yet have children, so it was easier for us than for those who had young children. There were no modern conveniences, like refrigerators. Beds, tables, chairs—everything had to be made out of materials we found in the woods. I'm not sure what they do today for Jungle Camp—or if they even still have it.

Before leaving for Jungle Camp, we were told we would all be moving to a different place upon returning from Jungle Camp, but we were not told where that would be. This was part of the training, too—learning to be flexible and keeping a good attitude. When we returned, we were moved to a room in the big dorm building rather than going back to the little cabin.

*****

The day came when our time at that training center was over. Our first baby was due within two weeks according to the doctor's calculations. I didn't like the doctor I had in Pennsylvania, so we decided to make a 1600 mile trip from Pennsylvania to Nebraska, where my parents lived at the time. I called my mom and asked her to make an appointment for me with her doctor for as soon as we arrived there. We ran into a heavy snowstorm leaving Pennsylvania; we followed a semi truck so we could know where we were going. The trailer we were pulling had two blowouts before reaching Wisconsin, where we stopped to see Fred's parents before continuing on to Nebraska.

Stephen Paul Sammons was born October 27, 1959, two weeks later than the doctor had calculated as the possible due date. He weighed in at 9 lbs. 2 oz. Fred wasn't in town. He was working on a cattle ranch sixty miles away to try to earn enough money to pay the hospital bill. He heard the announcement of Steve's birth on the radio and came into town to see me and the baby, but he was snowed in at the ranch the weekend I got out of the hospital. I went to my mom's and waited for him there.

Fred worked about three months on that cattle ranch where we lived in a small house; we enjoyed our time there. We became acquainted with ranchers from the area who attended a little Sunday School Union church not far from the ranch we were on. Fred ended up preaching there a lot. Some of those people became lifetime friends and supporters. When we were ready to go to Paraguay, that little church group paid our complete passage.

In January 1960, we entered the New Tribes Language Institute, which at that time was in Fredonia, Wisconsin. I was in the linguistic class and spent many late nights up studying, doing homework for the next day's class. We lived in a one-room apartment on the second floor of a dorm building. The public bathroom and running water were down the hall.

Fred's work detail during language school was working on cars—mostly for the staff. It was not unusual to find a carburetor apart on our table—our only table—in our small living quarters. That table was also our desk on which we did our studies. Although it was not a convenient setup, there wasn't much choice if I wanted to see more of my husband.

We finished our training in the language school that year just before the holidays and went to stay with Fred's parents until our second son, David James, was born on January 13, 1961. We then moved to a small dorm room at the New Tribes Bible Institute in Milwaukee to study Guarani with Duane Stous. He was on furlough and willing to teach those of us who had plans to go to Paraguay as missionaries.

The boys both got the hard measles while we were living in the dorm, but David was given gamma globulin shots to avoid taking a bad case because he was so little. (When he was fifteen, however, in Paraguay, he did get the hard measles again and said he felt like he was going to die. He was hospitalized because they broke out "inside" his body. A missionary nurse was staying with our kids at the time while Fred and I were in Brazil for a leadership conference representing the Field of Paraguay. We didn't know Dave was even sick until we returned from Brazil.)

*****

After completing the NTM training, we spent a year in North Platte, Nebraska, at my home church, where Fred became the visitation pastor. He was ordained by that church fellowship's council while we were living there. We lived up on the second floor of the church in a small apartment, which was next to the children's Sunday School classrooms. We were involved in leadership of the church's Primary Sunday School department and junior choir, served as pianist and secretary of the Navigator program of the church, did visitation, and helped wherever else we were needed.

The last day of February 1962, we left the United States for Paraguay, South America, on Braniff Airlines, arriving in Asunción on March 1, 1962. I was five months pregnant with our third child.

ASUNCIÓN PARAGUAY

1962

GUARANI LANGUAGE STUDY

Our first prayer card picture taken in 1961

2
ASUNCION, 1962

When we left North Platte, Nebraska, there was a wind chill factor of 40° Fahrenheit *below* zero. When we arrived in Paraguay the temperature was 40° Centigrade *above* zero, which is 104° Fahrenheit. It was hot and humid, and we were all dressed in suits. Back then, *everyone* dressed up to travel on international flights. The missionaries who met us at the airport in Asunción said, "Get those suit jackets and ties off those poor little boys."

Paraguay was considered a *hardship* country for those working for the American government in Asunción back then. We wouldn't consider it that today—at least not in the capital city where most of the American government people live. In 1962, the road from the airport into town wasn't yet paved; the street to the mission guesthouse was more like an oxcart trail. There were no supermarkets. We purchased groceries from little neighborhood stores or from women who went door to door selling garden produce on foot or on donkeys.

There were no ready-made clothes, though one could buy cheap material to make one's own clothes. Today one can buy imported clothing from Brazil, China, Korea, Argentina, and the United States, and nice clothing is made in Asunción as well. Packages could not be sent to us with any assurance we would receive them. Things were frequently stolen in the post office, so we told people to never send us anything.

The boys were one and two years old when we first went to Paraguay. We were thankful for our parents' blessing in our leaving for missionary service. Many others made comments like, "How can you take those poor little boys out to the mission field? Isn't it dangerous?" Others felt Fred was wasting his Moody education by being a missionary—as if missionaries didn't need an education.

Our answer to such remarks has always been that the safest place to be is in the center of God's Will—wherever that is. And we never had occasion to question His faithfulness to us over all those years of working in Paraguay.

"Therefore go and make disciples of all nations, baptizing them in the name of the Father and of the Son and of the Holy Spirit, and teaching them to obey everything I have commanded you. And surely I am with you always, to the very end of the age." Matthew 28:19-20

LANGUAGE STUDY

Paraguay is one of few countries with two recognized national languages—Spanish and Guarani. While Spanish is used in the capital city, specifically in business and education, Guarani is spoken by the majority of Paraguayans elsewhere in the country.

We were to spend at least six months in language study before being transferred to the interior to an Indian work; and as one can function almost anywhere in Paraguay speaking Guarani, it was the language of choice. Most Paraguayans were grateful we would learn their heart language. One could speak Spanish and have come from almost anywhere, but Guarani belonged to Paraguay. It was obvious one had made an effort to belong if one learned the Guarani language. Many of the indigenous people spoke Guarani as a trade language, and Guarani was the mother tongue for some of the indigenous tribes. Because the language study requirement was a bit heavy—and I was pregnant with our third child and had two little boys to care for at the same time—older missionaries insisted I needed a maid. So, against my wishes, we hired a lady from the neighborhood, who had come looking for work, to do the laundry. That was the most difficult job for me, as I had only a James washer.

Here's a picture of the James Washer. It was definitely better than no washing machine.

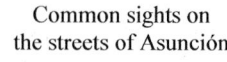

Pettirosi shopping

Common sights on the streets of Asunción

So Much for the Maid Idea!

We found out the woman who came to help with the work was stealing from us. Because I was much younger than she was and afraid to confront her, I got up at five o'clock in the morning and had the laundry done before she got there. When she came to work I told her I didn't need her anymore. On her way out of the house she stole the meat that I was going to cook for dinner, which was on the counter in the outdoor kitchen. So much for the *maid* idea!

One day while I was doing the laundry inside the tiny outdoor kitchen, I realized it was time to prepare lunch. All our meals were "one-dish" meals, frequently cooked in a pressure cooker on our only cook stove, a one-burner kerosene Primus. Pressure is pumped into the small tank, and alcohol is poured into a little tray to preheat it.

The burning alcohol was sold in glass liter bottles. While I was pouring the alcohol into the tray, the bottle slipped from my hands and broke all over the kitchen floor and splashed onto my feet. I had on "flip-flop" sandals while doing the laundry. I swept up the glass but didn't mop the floor, because I intended to mop it when the laundry was finished.

Paraguayan matches back then were about an inch long on waxed string; the sulfur tip often fell off when you struck the match. When I went to light the alcohol to start the Primus, the tip of the match fell on the floor, catching on fire both the floor and my feet, which were soaked with alcohol. I tried to run out of the kitchen but was caught on the wringer handle of the James washer and fell flat on my stomach out onto the adjoining porch—in my big pregnant state!

I hollered "Fred, help!" and no one showed up; I looked up to see the neighbor's gardener looking over the fence to see who was hollering. That was most embarrassing!

Fred finally showed up, and I asked why he didn't come when I called him. He said, "Oh, I figured you saw a rat, a big cockroach, a spider, or something." I soaked my feet in ice water for several hours and was uncomfortable for weeks. (Our Guarani teacher then told me to stay home from class to study and to help Fred with *his* lessons, as he said he knew I would get the language without difficulty. Little did I know how *that* prophecy was to become a reality!)

A missionary couple working in another location decided I needed a maid to help until the baby was born and sent a telegram saying, "Meet the TAM plane today. Juanita (fifteen years old) is coming to live with you and help with the work." She was arriving that very day! I didn't know her, had never met her or her family, and hardly had time to think about it. I'm sure I found time to cry. I didn't *want* someone else to come live with us, and I didn't want someone else doing my work!

Juanita had been living with the other missionary family, working for them; now she would be living with us. I didn't know what to expect. All I knew was that she was a country Paraguayan from a Christian family. I hadn't yet met her parents.

I was young—twenty-two, the youngest missionary on the field at the time—and new enough on the field that I was afraid to argue the situation with my elders. So Juanita came to live with us for about three months. I enjoyed doing my own house cleaning, so she did the laundry. There was plenty of that to do with little ones, and using the James washer wasn't exactly enjoyable for me while pregnant. We treated Juanita like one of the family, sharing the work. It was hard at first to get used to someone of a different culture living with us when we could barely communicate, but I learned a lot of Guarani from her, and we became good friends.

I preferred that Fred go to the bread store those first months, as I didn't like seeing the cockroaches running all over the shelves where the bread was kept. Choosing meat at the meat market wasn't exactly appetizing either. The lack of reasonable sanitary conditions was appalling.

Dora Grace was born June 28, 1962, in the Baptist Hospital in Asunción. It was a rather interesting experience having a doctor who spoke no English, and my Guarani was limited, but we managed to understand each other. Many of the same people who were on the hospital staff when Dora was born were still there when she was a patient, having her own last two babies in that same hospital, while serving as a missionary in Paraguay. Because of her nurse's training and experience after Bible school training, she was allowed more than once into surgery with an indigenous person who requested her presence. She accompanied many a new missionary to doctor's appointments as well.

Our First Winter in Asunción

There was no central heating or central air in any place we lived during all the years we lived in Paraguay. Considering how hot the summers are, it is amazing how cold it can be in the winters there. Both of the boys had asthma, and we had a hard time keeping them warm enough. We were all wearing winter jackets inside the house to try to keep warm.

After a week of the boys and I getting little sleep because of their asthma problems, we called a doctor. He changed their medication, thinking that might help, but he also stressed the need to get some warmth into the house at least part of the time. *How* were we to do that?

One thing a missionary must learn to do is to "makeshift"—be able to improvise with whatever is at hand. Failing to do so can bring a lot of frustration. Thankfully, that wasn't a problem for Fred. He didn't have an engineering degree, nor was he a professional carpenter, but he always managed to find a way to do whatever needed to be done. We made good use of more things that other people discarded than you can imagine.

Fred took a four-gallon oil can, laid it on its side, put some kind of frame under it, cut a hole on the underneath side where the one-burner Primus could be placed to heat up the oil can, and thus throw heat out the open end of the can. It was crude, but it worked.

Selling garden produce door to door on the streets of Asunción

Mbya Indian Contact

During the time we were in Asunción for Guarani study, Fred went on a trip with our field chairman, Duane Stous, and Alan Heckart, another older missionary, to make contact with an indigenous group of people called the *Mbya*. This group was living on the east side of Paraguay. The men soon found out the Mbya people weren't open to a visit from outsiders.

The three missionary men had borrowed horses from friends at a Swiss ranch and rode to within walking distance of the village where the Mbya people lived. They left the horses tied some distance away and hid their saddles and supplies in the woods.

As they approached the village, they saw people sitting outside their crude houses. Duane called in Guarani to announce their arrival. Immediately the people scattered, running into their homes. Duane told Fred and Alan to stand still and wait. Before they knew it they were surrounded on all sides by men with spears. The Mbya men had gone out the back of their houses and surrounded the three missionaries.

Duane talked to them in Guarani, explaining that they wanted to help them with education and medicine. For us to work in Paraguay with the indigenous people, the Paraguayan government required that we be involved in educating them, helping them medically, and whatever else we could do to improve their living conditions. That particular group of people had not been open to anyone helping them. They said they didn't need to learn to read and write, and they were not interested in help of any kind. They told the men to leave and never return, and if they did return, they would be killed. It's only been in recent years that these people have been open to any outside help. NTM is presently looking into the possibility of working with the Mbya in the near future.

The above picture shows us walking to a Sunday Indian meeting, where a few Lengua families living in the area met together to fellowship around God's Word. The picture below shows us in front of the house we lived in for four months, helping to "hold the fort" while another missionary family was on home assignment.

3
Lima Ty

When Dora was a couple of months old, we moved to the interior to a place called *Lima Ty* on the western side of the Paraguayan river, which is called the Chaco region. The country of Paraguay is divided right down the middle by the Paraguayan River, and the two sides are extremely different in climate and soil. The eastern side is lush and beautiful, and gardens flourish. It generally cools off at night, allowing for a decent night's rest, regardless of how humid or hot it may be during the day. The climate on the Chaco side is hot, dry, and buggy. It's a struggle to get anything to grow and is basically good only for cattle raising. Every biting bug you can imagine is content to live there and to bite you. It is definitely a more difficult place to live, physically. That is where we chose to serve. Did we know ahead of time it would be like that? No. But the need was great and the opportunity to serve likewise. Of course we were told it would be a hard place, but we didn't *sign up* for missionary work expecting it to be easy.

It was the Mennonites who opened up the Chaco initially. The Paraguayan government gave them freedom to live there on the condition that they develop the land. They were first to produce and develop many of the products the Paraguayans enjoy today. Many of the first Mennonite immigrants left Germany and Russia for Paraguay with only the clothes on their backs; many died of tuberculosis or leprosy, having suffered to make a better life for those who followed them. The Mennonites continue to be hard working and productive.

Introduction into Milking Cows

We were in Lima Ty for one month when the other family took a needed "break" to Asunción. They hadn't been off the station together as a family for a long time. Their previous co-workers were on furlough, and someone always had to remain present on the station. We were left alone to take care of things on the station for a month.

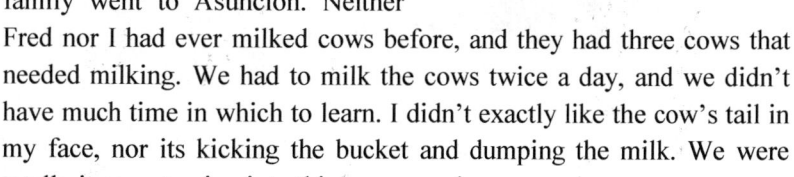

There were several new things for us to learn right away before this family went to Asunción. Neither Fred nor I had ever milked cows before, and they had three cows that needed milking. We had to milk the cows twice a day, and we didn't have much time in which to learn. I didn't exactly like the cow's tail in my face, nor its kicking the bucket and dumping the milk. We were totally ignorant going into this new experience.

One day it was raining, lightning, thundering, and fast getting dark. We took an Aladdin lamp into a small shelter where we also took the cows because of the rain. The cow closest to the lamp got scared and kicked the lamp over, breaking the mantle. I had to go back to the house quite a distance in the rain to get another mantle and try again. You'd think by then we'd have gotten smart and given up, but we didn't. Talk about *green*! We didn't realize we had an option. Rain or shine, we thought we had to be out there milking. Knowing what we know today, the little calves would have enjoyed the best meal they ever had on that rainy day!

Were we surprised the next day to find that all the milk was sour! All that work and hassle for nothing! The other missionary, upon return, told us we should never milk in a storm; it will always go sour. We didn't know. *Only in Paraguay?*

One of those cows had just had her first calf and wasn't used to being milked. After she kicked Fred in the mid-section a few times, he decided he wasn't going to milk her anymore. I certainly wasn't about to try. Fred told one of the Indians, "If you milk that cow while its owner is gone, you can have all the milk." That guy tried for about a week, then said, "I don't want any more milk." Guess what? We let that cow's calf suck until its owner returned. I'm sure that was one happy little calf.

INTRODUCTION TO "HANDS-ON" MEDICAL WORK

Although we had some Field Medicine study and a bit of practice giving injections (water shots into grapefruit and other students), we hadn't needed to do the "real" thing yet. However, an Indian man at Lima Ty had a badly ulcerated leg and had to have injections twice a day. We were left to continue the series of shots the other missionary had started.

We all walked over to the man's house one day with Fred to give the injection, and when we got there, Steve said, "Where's his house?" We were looking right at this little shack that certainly didn't look like a house. When we first moved to Lima Ty, Steve cried for several days, wanting to go *home* to Asunción. He didn't consider the place we lived a house either.

Typical Angaite Indian houses; the people on the right were more ambitious.

The "house" we lived in at Lima Ty was small and anything but private, with big screened window areas. It was rustic—a temporary shelter that had seen better days. The dirt floor was unleveled and full of holes, making it easy to trip and fall.

The cooking stove was made of mud bricks. Until I learned to make a good fire, Fred said he would make the first one of the day. But if I let it go out, tough luck; I had to rebuild the fire. Who would remember to keep a wood fire going all day in 100 degree heat? I had to restart the fire several times, but I learned to build a fire without it being a hassle. And the kids quickly adapted to primitive country living.

A fire incident took place at Lima Ty when someone got the kerosene and gas barrels mixed up, and some gas was evidently mixed into the kerosene barrel from which a kerosene Aladdin glass lamp was filled. I lit the lamp and it caught on fire. I was able to safely throw it out the door, but that was the end of a lamp I liked very much; it had belonged to my paternal grandparents.

One special memory Fred has of Lima Ty is hunting wild pig with a few of the Indians. He was supposed to be studying, but one of the Indians came up to the window and told him to hurry up and bring his gun; there were a lot of wild pigs out in the woods, and they wanted him to help get them. They had machetes, but no gun—and wild pigs can be dangerous.

When they got out into the woods, Fred noticed the Indians were all climbing trees or onto stumps to get off the ground. Fred was standing on the ground, and he soon found out why they weren't. The Indian dogs went in and scared up the herd of wild pigs, then ran back to their owners with the pigs chasing them. Fred quickly found a stump to stand on before they knocked him over. The short version of the story is—he shot three pigs.

Fred learned another thing *not* to do on that hunting trip. He tried to put those dead pigs up on a horse's back; that horse took one whiff of those pigs and was gone—without the pigs! So Fred and the Indians carried the pigs home as you can see in the photo on the next page. The Indians skinned and roasted those pigs and ate all three pigs in one day! The next day the three families were all lying around feeling awful.

The tendency of the poor indigenous people is to eat up all they have on hand, as they never know when they will have food like that again. They could make jerky out of some of it—but if they don't eat it all and there are other people around, they will be expected to give it away. The culture says you never refuse someone who asks you for food if you have anything at all to give.

By the time the hunter shares with all those who come begging from him, little or nothing is left for his own family. So when there is food, the tendency is for people to gorge themselves, making up for when there is no food. Not a healthy choice, but most of us cannot begin to relate to ever being as hungry as many of them have been—and often still are.

Fred loved going hunting with the Indians in his younger years. Generally, most, if not all of whatever he shot was given to the others who had gone with him. He later sold his gun and no longer hunted in the woods. He did do some fishing and alligator hunting in the river with the Indians in later years.

4
MOVE TO TUPÃRENDA

There were very few Indians in the Lima Ty area, so Fred and an associate did some checking around and found a big cattle ranch with headquarters at a place called Tupãrenda, which was central to hundreds of Angaite Indians who worked for the ranch. They asked permission to move there. The ranch boss was hesitant about our moving there initially, as he was *not* interested in having an evangelical preacher on the property—and he as much as said so; but he did give permission for us to build in an area on the other side of a swampy region, where we would be out of sight of the main ranch headquarters.

After getting permission to move to the ranch, Fred asked the ranch boss where he could get logs with which to build our house. The ranch boss gave Fred the name of someone to cut logs; so Fred contracted the individual, who said he would have the logs cut from the woods and brought in before Fred returned.

So in January 1963, we moved from Lima Ty to Tupãrenda. There were several outposts on the ranch that depended on the main headquarters for their monthly supplies of basic food items. These provisions were brought in by oxcart from a little town called Pinasco, a three-day oxcart trip one way. The trip was made once a month. Though we were allowed to purchase some basic things from their store once a month—of what was available—we were the last in line to be served.

The lower photo on the opposite page shows Fred and his helpers leaving Lima Ty for a place called Ceibo, where they met a wood-burning train on its very last trip. We were fortunate to get our belongings on it, as it passed within a reasonable distance from the ranch. That train was never in use thereafter. From the train line, our belongings were again put on oxcarts to finish the trip. Twelve oxen had to be used at one point because of the water, mud, and weight.

Fred moved with most of our things a couple weeks ahead of me, taking two Lengua men from Lima Ty with him to help with the move. His plan was to set up some kind of shelter before I went over with the three kids. He expected to find the contracted logs brought out of the woods waiting for him when he arrived at Tupãrenda.

But when Fred reached the specified location, there were no logs. Several Paraguayan families lived on the ranch and helped run it. Being strong Catholics, they did not want Protestant evangelicals on the property, and they hoped that by making things difficult for us, we would decide to leave and go elsewhere.

Regardless of the attitude of those trying to make things difficult for us so we would leave, we weren't about to give up that easy. After a few months when it became obvious there were no logs forthcoming, Fred talked to the Scottish ranch boss, who told the man who had been contracted to get the logs that he had better get them in soon or he would be sorry.

What we didn't realize until much later was that the palm logs the man finally brought were not of the harder type he was contracted to get, but we didn't know the difference until the sawdust kept sifting through from the bugs eating out the inside of the logs. There was nothing we could do about it. Fred would know the difference from now on.

I'm getting ahead of myself; I want to tell you about my initial arrival to Tupãrenda with the three kids just two weeks after Fred had arrived there with our things.

My Arrival at Tupãrenda with the Three Kids

One day when Fred knew the mission pilot was flying to Lima Ty with supplies, he got on the radio he had taken with him and said to the pilot, "Bring Ruthie and the kids over today." The pilot asked, "Are you sure you're ready for Ruthie and the kids to be there? Is there a place for them to stay?" "Yeah, sure, it's all ready." (Said Fred!)

We had to grab up everything in a hurry to leave on short notice. Elías, a Lengua man, was there visiting and helped me grab the clothes off the clothesline and get whatever things we had left to take to the plane—and off we went on a new adventure.

And a new adventure it was! We got off the plane and onto an oxcart to be taken across a swamp to where we would be living. It was hot, muggy, and super buggy with polverines (no seeums) thick as all get out. I had never seen so many bugs in my life, and they were all biting! All I could think was, *These poor little kids are going to be eaten up alive!*

Fred was thrilled to see us, but he could see *I* had some questions. He said, "What's the matter? Aren't you happy to be here? We've always been willing to rough it to be together rather than being apart." My response: "But where are the kids going to sleep, and what if it rains?"

He had found an old broken down shed on the property, made of slats of old palm, which he took apart and used to put together a shelter of a sort. BUT it had no roof on it! When I asked, "What if it rains?" Fred and the others laughed, as there wasn't a cloud in the sky. So the mattresses were put down on the dirt floor of the shed. We had no idea at that time that we'd be living outdoors for five more months. Nor was I yet aware that we would be encountering poisonous snakes, tarantulas, scorpions, and who knows how many other kinds of *bichos* on a regular basis.

Well, it rained the very first night the kids and I were there. Everything we had was soaked, and so were we. Thereafter a "makeshift" roof, which included my plastic tablecloth, covered the shed until other materials were available. We put all our belongings inside to keep them from being ruined. We slept outside, making a bed under a big tree—with a tarp over us when it rained. I made a large mosquito net out of the baby's Curity diapers, and we all slept together under the same net.

We suspected our designated living site was given so we wouldn't *contaminate* the Paraguayans with our message or influence their lifestyle, but it turned out to be an excellent location. The Paraguayans told us we were in the path of the jaguars. We did hear a jaguar occasionally, and one night a jaguar killed forty sheep over by the main headquarters. But with all the animals on the ranch, we felt we were probably safe. That was our hope and prayer at least.

Why did we move in rainy season? First of all because the train that was available for part of the move was on its very last trip. The other reason? The unpredictability of the rainy season's timing. It seemed it was rainy season every time we made a major move—and it never seemed to fall at the same time of year. The Chaco doesn't normally get much rain, but we sure got plenty of it those first few months we were living outside. Is it any wonder when people in the United States get excited about camping, we just smile and think "more power to them"? We've already encountered all the camping we care to experience.

We had a kerosene refrigerator that sat for a few months not being used, because the Paraguayans on the ranch refused to sell us enough kerosene, saying there was none available.

We were still using a one-burner kerosene Primus as Fred didn't yet have materials to build the brick wood-burning stove. There were a few times we didn't have enough kerosene to use the Primus, and because of heavy rain it was impossible to build a fire to cook. That happened only a few times; we always had dry hardtack biscuits and powdered milk.

The ranch boss felt sorry for us with all the rains and no house, so he eventually sent over a tent we could put things in to keep dry. If it rained hard, we could sleep in the tent, but it was so hot and muggy we preferred to sleep outside whenever possible.

We finally moved from sleeping under the tree to sleeping under a roof, which later became a porch off the storage shed. Fred figured out where the walls of our house would be (before we got the logs), ordered bricks from the company store and built a wood-burning stove where the kitchen was to be located, even though there wasn't a roof over it yet. He used two-thirds of a two-hundred-liter barrel to make an oven, and it worked super. I became very adept at making bread, cakes, and everything else in that barrel oven; by then I knew how to start a decent wood fire and control it. The picture below was taken after the house was built around the stove.

Outdoor Sleeping, all in one bed under a tarp.

It was five months before we were in our house. It was rustic, but we felt very at home in it. We didn't yet have mud between the cracks of the palm logs when we moved in, and the floor was loose dirt for a couple years, but it was *home,* and it was *ours.*

After a couple of years, a deep hole was dug in the hope of making a cistern in which to hold the rainwater—but it didn't work. We didn't have available what we needed to keep the walls from caving in. Thus, the rainwater off the tin roof was channeled into metal drums that were each capable of holding two-hundred liters of water.

The clay from that hole was good for making a decent floor, so we mixed it to spread on top of the dirt floor. As we were doing that, Fred got an awful gallbladder attack and was unable to help, so Juancito (an Angaite man) and I put in the clay floor throughout the whole house, walking it out to try to level it as best we could.

Because of the extreme heat in the Chaco, the house was built with windows directly across from each other so that prevailing winds could blow through the house. And with all those windows, we also had lots of eyes watching us from dawn until dark. That was hard to get used to.

We were the first missionaries to live there. The Indians were told we were there to help them; they were suspicious of our intentions initially. Why would we help them if we weren't personally benefiting somehow?

Once we were in our house, the ranch boss moved the whole Indian village over near us. The mission airstrip was the only thing that separated us from them. Our closest neighbors were within a stone's throw of our house; so we had more people than ever watching everything we did.

I was teased about how often I swept that dirt floor; someone said thirteen times a day. That was a big exaggeration, but I did sweep it after every meal. I sprinkled the floor with the rinse water from doing the dishes (in dishpans). We had no sink or running water, and I never left dirty dishes waiting, or there would soon be ants, cockroaches, and *who knows what else* making themselves at home in our kitchen. All dirty dishwater was poured on the plants or trees, as was the laundry and bath water. The clean rinse water was sprinkled on the floor. Water was never just thrown out for nothing.

Dampening and sweeping the floor immediately after meals not only kept down the dust and bugs, it also kept the clay from cracking. The kids were made to wipe their feet at the door before coming in. We put throw rugs in front of the beds and made the rustic house look homey.

At least once a week I moved all the furniture to clean behind and under it, often rearranging it. I was teased about that by co-workers, but it was a good way to keep down the rats, mice, and snakes. Fred said I at least kept them confused.

The Indian village being moved over near us proved to be a blessing in time. The exception was hearing the constant noise of the drums accompanying the drinking and dancing going on all night long, night after night as they attempted to appease the evil spirits. The next day people would come begging for aspirin for their splitting headaches.

It was sometimes hard to feel merciful towards those who were suffering hangovers and those who had wounds that needed treated because of the fights they got into, because someone slept with someone else's wife—a common result of the dances. Alcohol and immorality were always associated with the dancing. Is it any wonder I find it hard to understand the acceptance today of dancing and drinking of alcoholic beverages at Christian social events in this country?

Our first year at Tupãrenda was the hardest, because we didn't yet have friends among the people there—neither Indians, nor nationals. Though we bought some of our staples from the company store on the ranch, we tried to have a plane flight once a month for vegetables and other items. The Paraguayans would tell us there would be flour and sugar at the store, so we would not order it on the flight from Asunción, but when the supplies arrived to the ranch by oxcart, there often would not be flour, sugar or kerosene for us, and it was too late to order the things we wanted on the flight. We shared the flight with our co-workers (who had also moved to Tupãrenda some weeks after we had moved there); flight costs were calculated on how much kilo weight we each had brought in.

The staples we bought from the ranch store were often full of weevils and other bugs, as the company in Pinasco would keep the newer supplies they received from the boats that came upriver from Asunción and send on the old provisions to the ranch. There was no worry about preservatives in the food—there wasn't any such thing.

We tried to grow a vegetable garden. It was difficult partly because of the bugs, but also because of the extreme weather changes. One year we planted three times, losing everything once from a flood, another time from drought and a third time from hail.

We did have an Indian man work in the garden when there was a garden to work in. One day he came drunk, and when he was told to weed the garden, he pulled up all the lettuce and threw it out. At that time the Indians didn't even know what lettuce was; it looked like weeds to them.

At Tupãrenda we had no electricity. We did later buy a used Maytag wringer washing machine with Briggs & Stratton gas engine from missionaries who were returning to the United States. That sure made the laundry easier. For lights we used Aladdin lamps initially; we later got a gas pressure lantern. For ironing clothes, I first used sadirons heated on top of the wood stove, then graduated to a charcoal iron, then later replaced that with a gas pressure iron—*none of which I recommend*.

Fred made a couch from cowhide stretched over poles cut from the jungle; the kids were taught that whatever we had, no matter how cheap or crudely made, it was to be treated with respect. We never had to be afraid of them mistreating anyone else's furniture when we were on furlough.

In time we became good friends with the Scottish ranch boss and his family—their children were close to the ages of our kids. They proved to be some of the best neighbors we ever had. They moved to Brazil around the same time we were transferred to another location. We have continued to keep in touch by mail all these years.

This is a view from our back door when we got up early in the morning.

It wasn't long before we had people asking us to help them with their medical needs. There was a high percentage of active TB in the village. Thus we brought in TB meds, started a vaccination program for the children, and vaccinated the pregnant women with tetanus vaccine. Many babies had died of tetanus prior to our arrival. We lost no babies of vaccinated mothers to tetanus all the time we worked in Paraguay.

These people didn't have birth certificates or any means of personal identification. Most of them do now. Until a kinship analysis was done later on, and birth records kept, their exact age was uncertain in most cases. Even now, there are mothers who don't remember their children's birthdates; but those who are working as health promoters among their own people are now keeping track of birth and vaccination records.

There is now more of an effort on the part of the Paraguayan government to see that the indigenous people have identification cards as well as birth certificates. There was a time when no one seemed to care whether they lived or died.

Dora and Debbie are watching me give a child an injection. Both of the girls did medical work years later when they returned to Paraguay as missionaries.

Debra Lynn was born November 24, 1964. More will be said regarding her birth in the next chapter.

We caught rainwater off the tin roof for drinking and used the swamp water for baths, cleaning, laundry, and so on. But when the rainwater ran out, we had to drink the swamp water which had to be boiled; sometimes it smelled so bad I didn't want to drink it even after it was boiled. Before using the swamp water for anything, we first stirred alum into it to settle the dirt to the bottom of the barrel. When the swamp was dry, it meant going a distance away by buckboard to the cattle's water hole.

Speaking of water shortages, our kids today think it's unbelievable that when they were small at Tupãrenda, they all had to bathe in the same tub of bathwater, from the cleanest kid to the dirtiest. Because of the heat and playing outdoors, they bathed twice a day—midday for lunch, followed by a nap; then again in the evening for supper, when they were ready for bed. The water was emptied out onto plants or trees where needed after the last kid had a bath. When they got older, they took bucket showers and learned to do so in half a bucket of water. Fred put a hole in the bottom of a metal bucket, attached a showerhead, pulled the bucket up on a rope attached to a pulley on one of the rafters—and ready to go. We used that kind of shower for as long as we lived in the interior.

Dora obviously wants to help with the laundry. The boys are playing with Indian friends in our yard.

The boys liked to go hunting with Fred. Dave's sharp eyes often spied the game before his dad did.

The kids are playing in the swamp in front of our house—before we were aware of alligators in there.

Fred went bird hunting while we were fishing; he got tired of baiting my hook.

There was a lot of racial discrimination against the Indians by the country Paraguayans. Though it still exists somewhat, it's not to the extent that it used to be. We were asked, "Why do you bother to treat those people for TB? They don't have a soul; they're just like animals." And sadly, many of the Paraguayans at the time believed that. Such sentiments are slowly changing today, thankfully.

"For whosoever shall call upon the name of the Lord shall be saved. How then shall they call on Him in whom they have not believed? and how shall they believe in Him of whom they have not heard? and how shall they hear without a preacher? And how shall they preach, except they be sent?..." Romans 10:13-15a

5
MORE TUPÃRENDA EXPERIENCES

Health situation of the people at Tupãrenda.

An American doctor from the Baptist hospital in Asunción came to check out the TB situation among the Indians. He told us to never have Indian household help because both of our boys had asthma, and they would be sure to catch TB with their weak lungs. The doctor found that 80 percent of the indigenous people living at Tupãrenda had *active* tuberculosis.

One woman who had the worst TB, coughing up blood, etc., was always wanting to pick David up when we first moved there. I would just turn my head and pray, as I didn't dare offend her by taking him away. He fussed enough that she would put him back down quickly. None of us ever contracted TB, though we were around it and treating it constantly.

There were times we were offered "tereré" (a Paraguayan tea drunk through a shared metal straw) by people we knew had TB, but we dared not offend them. We just prayed God would protect us. Those people had no knowledge whatsoever of "germs" and how they were contracted. We did our best to teach them, but it took many years before most even believed us. They felt that sickness came from the evil spirits.

Cultural beliefs such as this are difficult to change. It has taken many years for even a minority of them to realize that many diseases are contagious and they may be avoided or lessened through vaccinations and basic sanitation.

We didn't try to expose ourselves to TB. We took what precautions we could, but we chose not to offend—but to trust the Lord for His protection, in order to win the hearts of those people—letting them know we really cared for them. If people don't trust or like you, they won't listen to your message either.

I'll never forget one of the first women we treated for TB. Her name was Susana. Her family had given up her ever recovering and just left her off in a room alone to die. As she was in no condition to care for herself, death was inevitable. Many had already died of TB before our arrival there. We started giving her injections along with the TB pills, pouring broth in her mouth, as she was too weak to eat. To everyone's amazement Susana started responding.

The most joyous part of this story is that she later was the first woman to accept the Lord as her Savior. We had a visiting doctor check her once, and he said her lung needed to be collapsed, so she needed to go out for surgery. She refused to leave her family to do that, and she lived another fifteen years before she died. She never got rid of the TB, but it was under control with continued medication. Today they have better medicines for tuberculosis, and the claim is the TB can actually be cured if the treatment is followed correctly.

A picture of Susana is on the opposite page. She had several miscarriages because of her sickness; pregnancies were hard on her, but she was able to raise three sons.

One of the first things we tried to do at Tupãrenda was to teach literacy and arithmetic. The indigenous people there had never been taught to read or write. The children weren't allowed to attend school with the national children. Those who had outside jobs were often cheated by their employers because they didn't know their money or the kilo weights of the food they bought. They weren't so easily fooled once they learned the difference, and there was no quicker way to teach math to an uneducated person than by using money and *playing store*. We were not exactly appreciated by the nationals back then for educating these people.

LACK OF PRIVACY

For the first few years we had Indians looking in every window, watching our every move from sunup till sundown. It wasn't just children, either. I found it frustrating as I couldn't even bathe the baby without several people watching, and I felt stupid as they watched me talking to the baby (like we Americans do) while I bathed her. No matter what I was doing, I had an audience. It was most difficult to have people staring at us as we ate our meals. There was no way we could share our food with five hundred people.

One day I mentioned to an older co-worker how frustrating it was to me to be watched all day long, every day. She said, "Just think, Ruthie, what they're learning as they watch you bathe the baby, scrubbing the kids' heads, washing dishes with hot soapy water, etc. It's good for them to see you do those things." Frankly, it didn't seem to make much impression on most of them as far as an example to follow. Their kids' heads were often caked with scabs from lice, sometimes full of maggots that needed to be treated. Dirty faces didn't seem to bother them in the least. And they certainly couldn't understand what we wanted to be private about.

I did make curtains that could be pulled shut for the bedroom windows and for places where we might desire some privacy at certain times of the day or night. Later on, we had new co-workers, rather newlywed, who weren't used to being on display all day long, and it made them nervous. So they left in the plastic windows we all used to snap in (on the outside) when it was cold or raining. People started tearing the plastic on their windows, trying to see in, wondering what they were trying to hide.

Americans overall like their privacy, so this is a big adjustment for those of us living in Indian villages where people do not respect privacy the way we think of respecting privacy. I often wondered how they handled having so many people living in one room, changing clothes in front of the opposite sex without embarrassment. It took years before I realized they were far more curious about what you were trying to "hide" if you tried to be sneaky about changing clothes off in a corner somewhere. They just changed clothes right in the middle of the room, if need be, and no one made anything of it. That is another reason why we didn't allow our children to run free in the village or go on their own inside the Indian houses.

Emergency Flight—1963

One day, when Dora Grace was one year old, David was two and a half, and Steve not yet four years old, we decided to go visit the ranch boss's family. The kids liked going horseback riding and enjoyed the opportunity to play with the ranch boss's kids.

It was late afternoon when we got back to our house. Fred had evidently left his thyroid medication on the kitchen table; I hadn't noticed it, and when he went to get it, he couldn't find it. He asked me, "Ruthie, did you see my thyroid medicine? I can't find it anywhere." I asked, "Where did you leave it?" To which he said, "I think I must have left it right here on the table."

I hadn't seen his medicine, so we asked the boys, "Did you happen to see Daddy's medicine that was on the table?" Right away, one of them said, "We didn't waste any," and admitted to eating the pills. So we asked them to show us where they went to eat the medicine. They took us out to the yard where they had sat down to divide the pills between the two of them, insisting they hadn't wasted any. We asked, "Did they taste good?" David said, "They were such pretty little pills."

Our pilot was on radio three times a day in case there were an emergency, so at 6:00 p.m. I called in to let him know that the boys had eaten ninety thyroid pills between them. I had no idea if it was serious or not and asked if he could please find out if there was something we should do about it. He said, "Be back on the radio in one hour; meanwhile I will call the Baptist hospital and find out."

When we turned the radio back on, the pilot said it was urgent to get the boys into Asunción before twenty-four hours were up as their hearts could stop. It had already been at least six hours since the boys had swallowed the pills; it was too late to make a flight that night. They told us to try to get them to vomit, give something to cause diarrhea—anything to try to get that medication out of their system, but it was too late. Nothing worked.

The pilot said we needed to get a flight out as early as possible the next morning. The mission plane was down for maintenance and inspection. They asked us to try to hire the company plane of the ranch corporation, but it was not available, either. As it turned out, Brownie (our NTM pilot at the time) rented another plane for us, and he piloted it.

As we arrived into Asunción, Steve started vomiting. We took the boys directly to the Baptist hospital to be checked by a Southern Baptist missionary doctor. He told us all the terrible things that could happen to the boys—like do all their growing in one year, or end up with big goiters. I have forgotten the other possibilities. It was all rather scary.

The doctor said the kids would be super hyper from the thyroid medication, and he put them on Phenobarbital. He said it would take two weeks before we would know what the outcome might be and how much damage was done. During that two weeks their pulse needed to be monitored several times a day. He gave me a stethoscope to keep check on them; if the pulse got beyond a certain point, we were to rush them to the hospital. We had to take Steve in twice.

To everyone's surprise, the doctor was so concerned he came to the mission guesthouse several evenings to check on the boys. Those doctors were not known to make house calls.

What we then found out was that the evening we called in by radio, asking if the situation was serious, the ACA (Asunción Christian Academy) was having a board meeting. Present at that board meeting were members from several different mission boards, most of whom *we* didn't even know. Dr. Skinner was at that meeting and explained to the others the possible complications that could arise from the boys eating the thyroid medication. They had a prayer meeting right there for the boys.

For a long time afterwards we had people in Asunción from other mission boards asking about our kids. They had all been praying for them. We know that God answered their prayers! None of the ugly things happened that could have happened as a result of the boys eating that medication.

This may sound strange to some people, but we believe God may have allowed that emergency to take place so we would be in Asunción with Dora Grace. At the same time we were monitoring the boys, Dora became very sick with infectious diarrhea. It's the disease that more kids die of in Paraguay than any other illness. She had an ear infection we didn't even realize she had. She ended up hospitalized for four days, fed intravenously through her foot. The doctor said that had we not already been in Asunción, we probably would have lost Dora, as she dehydrated so fast. They asked us at the hospital not to stay with her, as they had problems with parents interfering when kids needed injections, not wanting the child to be wakened for medications, and so on.

They kept Dora drugged so she was kind of "out of it." We went to the hospital every day and peeked through the window to see how she was but didn't let her see us. One day we took a little stuffed animal and placed it in her arms without her seeing us. She immediately tried to see who was there, but we weren't allowed to let her see us. That was hard on this mother, believe me!

The American chaplain's eighteen-year-old son used to go in and talk to her and pick her up as he felt sorry for her. The hospital personnel made him quit, because they said she cried more afterwards.

We thanked God that, though we could have lost all three of our kids in a matter of a couple weeks, He spared their lives and saved them from ugly complications as well. God is so good!

God's Faithful Protection

There were other times we were very much aware of God's hand at work protecting our family members and others in our total ignorance of any danger. I'm thinking of a couple of incidents that had to do with Fred and his gun.

Our kids routinely took naps after lunch. They were always required to lie down for a certain amount of time and be quiet whether they slept or not. As the boys got bigger they didn't necessarily sleep; they could look at a book, but they had to be on their beds and quiet until we told them it was time to get up. One day, the boys had gotten up and had gone outside to play. We thought Dora, a toddler, was still taking a nap.

It was very rare for Fred to shoot anything in our yard apart from poisonous snakes, but that day he saw a toucan bird in a fruit tree and went out to shoot it. We didn't eat the birds Fred shot if there was an Indian nearby who needed the food. I don't remember Fred ever shooting another toucan after that day. When Fred shot at the bird, he saw it fall into the swamp reeds in front of our house. The toucan has a bright red-orange beak and a black body. Fred could see the orange and black colors in the reeds and was getting ready to shoot again to be sure the bird didn't get away before he retrieved it, but he felt checked about pulling the trigger.

I have always been grateful for the fact that when Fred feels checked about something, he checks things out before acting. When he felt checked about pulling the trigger, he thought, "This is ridiculous," but then felt checked again. So he went down to the edge of the swamp to see why he couldn't shoot.

There lay Dora Grace, sound asleep. Evidently she had followed the boys outside and fell asleep there in the swamp reeds. The boys weren't aware she had followed them. She was wearing the exact same colors as that toucan. Fred picked her up and brought her into the house, really shaken as he told me what happened. We thanked God immediately for His protection.

Another time Fred and an Indian man were hunting out in the woods, thinking no one else was around. They saw movement behind tall grass and thought an animal was coming out. They were ready to shoot, when the moving "being" started singing in Guarani, "I have decided to follow Jesus."

The day I was stung by a big scorpion, I was thankful it didn't get one of the kids. A scorpion sting in Paraguay can be fatal for small children. It took seven hours with my foot packed in ice before the pain lessened. Many years later I was stung again by a scorpion on my hand. The pain took many hours to subside, no matter what I tried; that time I didn't have access to ice.

An even scarier thing had happened to me when we weren't yet moved into the house. Fred had gone hunting, and when he returned, he leaned his .22 rifle up against a hardwood pole. He thought he had put the gun on safety, but without us being aware of it, Steve walked up and (without lifting the gun) pulled the trigger. The long rifle shell hit a hardwood crosspiece that was helping hold up the porch roof and ricocheted right through my hair! Needless to say, that was one time I was glad to be only five feet tall! From then on, the shells were always removed immediately from the gun when hunting was over!

Snakes

Oh yes, there were a lot of snakes where we built our house. The area was full of brush, weeds, and tall grass that had to be cut back and cleared. It was a great place for snakes to hide. We probably killed more "yarara" (fer-de-lance) snakes that first year or so than you can imagine. They are an extremely poisonous snake.

One day while we were still living outside, with beds under a roof but no walls, the boys were playing with baby Dora and bouncing around a bit on the bed which made the mattress start to slide off. I told the kids, "Don't bounce on that bed!" I decided to go put the mattress back in place; and when I did, I was amazed to see a yarara snake coming up between the elastic springs of the bed, right where the mattress was sliding off. He would soon have been right up with the kids! I first carefully removed the kids, and then killed the snake. *God was always so good to protect us.*

Another night, while still sleeping outside, I had put the kids to bed, and for some reason I was looking for Steve's shoes. I looked everywhere but couldn't find them, when, all of a sudden I saw a large coiled rattlesnake. I hollered at Fred and he got his gun. He told me to hold a flashlight on the snake. It must have mesmerized the snake. I didn't know at the time that they can throw themselves when coiled; I was *not* very far away from him.

We had fallen heir to an old piano that was left in the place we lived at Lima Ty, and the snake was near that piano. Fred didn't want to shoot into the piano, so he climbed on top of a dresser, telling me to hold the light on the snake. I kept saying, "Hurry up and shoot that thing!" He said, "Well, I'm trying to get in position to not hit the piano!" Finally he did shoot it. That was a bit scary. (That piano was later given to another missionary, whose house later burned down along with the piano.)

God obviously had me looking for Steve's shoes. With all the snakes we saw at that place, none of us were ever bitten. We had to tell the boys to let their dad know when they saw a snake so they could watch him shoot it. Otherwise, they would chase after them, which was dangerous. I refused to shoot a gun; I used a machete or a hoe to kill such creatures.

One day, long after we were moved into our house, David walked into the house carrying a small coral snake by the tail. "Look at this pretty little snake; it looks like beads," was his comment. I said, "Get that thing out of here and back outside where you got it and kill it." One of our co-workers was present at the time and said, "You're sending that kid back out with that snake?" I said, "He brought it in, he can take it out!"

Another time Fred walked into the laundry room where I was showering, and said, "I like your friend, but don't move. You are taking a shower with a coral snake." He killed it.

More than once, before I knew better, I tried to help crying little frogs out of cracks between the logs of our house, or out from under the fridge; and when I couldn't get them, I said, "Well, you stupid little thing. If you want to stay in that crack, just stay there." Then one day, an older co-worker saw me and said: "Ruthie, get away from there and leave that frog alone; there's a snake attached to it." Thereafter, I knew that when I heard a frog cry, there was also a snake attached. I would often run to where I heard the frog, hoping I could kill the snake before it dragged the frog into a hole in the ground, but often I couldn't get there fast enough.

Another day I was cooking or doing dishes when the co-worker walked in and said, "Ruthie, don't move; there's a coral snake going between your feet." At such times it's tempting to move anyway, but one realizes the safest thing to do is to *do as you're told*.

There's a lot more that could be said about snakes. I don't want to bore you with too many snake stories, but there are a couple more that come to mind that I will never forget.

One event happened while we were living outdoors, soon after arriving to Tupãrenda. Fred had to go somewhere on horseback for some business and was gone several hours. He came back toward evening, and while we were sitting down eating supper, he said, "Oh, I've got to get that snake out of the suitcase." I said, "*What* snake?" He said, "Oh this morning I was in a hurry and I didn't have time to kill it. I saw a yarara in the suitcase, but because I was in a hurry I just closed it up in the suitcase to kill it later."

I said, "You have got to be kidding! I moved that suitcase several times today while trying to rearrange and work with some of our stuff. How did you know I wouldn't open that suitcase?" All he said was, "Well, you didn't, right? So what's the big deal?" Well, you can imagine it was a big deal to me!

"Be still and know that I am God."
Psalm 46:10

Behind where I was teaching the literacy class (in the photo below) was our bedroom in the hot weather. It was attached to the house, screened on three sides. If we wanted privacy, we put down those shades made out of swamp reeds. The room had a split palm roof where sometimes the snakes or rats made themselves at home.

In time, that roof acquired a hole in it where it could rain in and obviously needed repair. I asked Fred to fix it—but it wasn't that urgent, right? It didn't rain that often in the Chaco, maybe once a month if we were lucky.

When he was on a trip somewhere, and I was sleeping out there by myself, I got up very early one morning to go to the bathroom or to take care of one of the kids; and when I came back to get in bed, there was a poisonous snake in my bed. I pulled back the covers to climb in, and there it was. Thankfully it was light enough for me to see it, and I was able to kill it. (Sometimes snakes would get away. It was not a good feeling, when that happened.) Fred fixed the roof when he got home.

*Let God have your life;
He can do more with it than you can.*

Surgery for Fred

While I was pregnant with our fourth baby, Fred had to be flown out to Asunción for gallbladder surgery. We had already known he had a gallbladder problem, but the doctor said he needed to be built up physically before they could do the surgery. Meanwhile I was to give him morphine shots whenever he had a bad attack.

I was careful to not fix anything he couldn't eat. But after a while, the kids started asking why I didn't make cookies or brownies like our co-workers. I felt sorry for the kids, so one day I decided to make them some brownies. I put them on top of the refrigerator, out of sight so Fred wouldn't see and eat them. Well, they were out of *my* sight—I'm much shorter than Fred, and though I couldn't see them, he could. And you guessed it, he got into them, even though he knew he shouldn't and had a terrible attack. I did give in and give him the injection he was supposed to have for such an attack, and he didn't cheat again on his diet.

When it was inevitable that surgery had to be done, I stayed on the station with the family while Fred flew to Asunción for the operation. An x-ray showed a stone stuck in the duct, so they expected complications. They waited a few days on the surgery, hoping the stone would pass. A Paraguayan who was a neighbor to the mission guesthouse told Fred to drink a particular herbal tea and gave him the leaves to make it. It worked. They were able to do the surgery, removing the stones without complications, but it wasn't a fast recovery. They had removed over one hundred stones.

I got a radio call, asking me to make the trip to Asunción with the family to take care of Fred as he needed more care than previously expected. He was very weak after the surgery. Back then they kept people in the hospital longer than they do today; and because of all the infection, he had a drain attached to him for a few weeks. He was bent over and looked like an old man, but he was young (in his late twenties), so it didn't take long to get back his strength.

Note of Interest Concerning Fred's Gallbladder Problem

Before Fred's surgery, after he had been teaching the Angaite people for some time, he was doing a series on Satan. Every Saturday night, during his preparation for that series, he would have a terrible gallbladder attack; consequently, he was too weak to present the message on Sunday. The other co-worker wasn't fluent enough in the language to substitute for him. Finally, one day when Fred was very sick with another gallbladder attack, the co-workers came over to talk with us and said they felt we all needed to make it a real matter of prayer, because it was obvious that the enemy was using this to disallow the teaching. We did pray together—praying that Fred would be strong enough to put the message on tape, which he did; the other missionary played the tape the next day at the meeting. No more gallbladder attacks on Saturday night.

Opposition from Witchdoctors

Because we were caring for the sick, and they were getting well, the five witchdoctors decided that Fred was just another witchdoctor like themselves, but stronger—and ruining their work. They didn't like the teaching of God's Word. They got together doing their dance and calling on the evil spirits to try to put a curse on Fred to kill him; but they said a spirit answered them saying, "We can't touch him; he has a stronger spirit protecting him." That story we learned later from the first man in the village who accepted the Lord.

The witchdoctors told the people that the injections I gave the sick were going to kill them. There was a very sick man who wanted my help, but every time I went to care for him, some witchdoctors walked out of the house. I took another Angaite with me as a witness and told the family that they had to make a choice—either the witchdoctors would treat him, or I would. The witchdoctors often used poison from the jungle and actually killed people; they could then blame me. So I refused to take care of the man while they refused to make a choice.

Later, when that man was strong enough to walk, he came and asked me to medicate him again—saying it was not *his* choice to have the witchdoctors, it was his people's. I was then able to help the man.

The power of evil oppression was often so prevalent when we walked into some of those houses that we about passed out. We would go back outside immediately and pray for God's protection over our lives and over the lives of those we were treating. People who had been told bad things about evangelicals would often spit to show their opposition to us. But the sick were grateful for our help.

Linguistic analysis for the American Bible Society

While living at Tupãrenda, I was asked to do a grammatical linguistic analysis of Guarani in English for the American Bible Society. I was also on the checking committee for checking the orthography when the New Testament was first printed. There were some Guarani grammars written in Spanish by some Catholic priests, who were anthropologists, but there was so much variation between them on the orthography, that the Bible Society requested a linguistic analysis in English to give them a basis for establishing principles for the orthography of the New Testament translation.

I was pregnant with Debbie and nearly miscarried several times while working on the linguistic analysis for the Bible Society. We found out when Deb was born what the problem was: She was a placenta previa baby, so any extra strain or stress on my body caused for the contractions to begin. She was born by Caesarean section after an unbelievable number of hours of labor. Fortunately, we were already in Asunción, because I had flown out a few weeks earlier with contractions five minutes apart, making the pilot very nervous. Fred and the boys joined me and Dora in town when the possibility of surgery was mentioned. Our co-workers figured he'd be little good to them what with worrying about me.

Debra Lynn was born November 24, 1964. We were happy with our two boys and two girls and glad to get back to the station; but after one month back home in the interior, I ended up back in the hospital with a fever and bad infection that left me with pain for a long time after. The doctor said I needed a hysterectomy, but given the fact that I was only 25 years old, he decided not to do it. He said to wait until I couldn't handle the pain any longer; so five years later we changed hospitals and doctors and had the necessary surgery.

Medical emergency for Debbie

When Debbie was just one year old she broke out with a siege of boils, five of them on her bottom. I soaked her in Epsom salts and drained two of them, but three of them refused to drain, so we gave her a penicillin injection. The Keefes were our co-workers at the time; Linda, a registered nurse, gave the first injection—moms don't like "sticking" their own kids, after all, though I had to do plenty of it later.

That same day, we flew to Asunción to attend our annual field conference. That conference was one of two that I was privileged to attend our first five years on the field, though Fred was able to attend them all. In those days, it was required by the Indian department that someone always had to remain on the station.

One of the missionaries in town had a doctor's appointment that day, so I said, "Please ask the doctor if he would give me a prescription for long-acting penicillin, because I've tried to find it and can't get it." The person returned, saying, "The doctor said Debbie is too young for long-acting penicillin, just keep using what you already started with."

The following day I went shopping, while Fred stayed with the children at the mission guesthouse. When I returned, I saw that Debbie had what looked like mosquito bites all over her. I said to Fred, "Why is this baby all bit up with mosquito bites?" He said, "There aren't any mosquitoes."

It was time for Deb's 2nd penicillin injection, so I gave it to her, and in a very few minutes she was swollen up like a balloon—hardly recognizable as the same person. There was no telephone at the guesthouse at that time, but the administrator lived on the property and *just happened* to be on the radio with the pilot at the time, who did have a phone. The administrator asked the pilot to call the hospital for us; they said to get to the hospital as quickly as possible.

The doctor said he wasn't sure if Deb would make it or not, so he asked that one of us stay with her. I stayed. He then said to me, "You might not want to see this." I said, "I do. I need to know what to do if we have an Indian react to penicillin." To that, he said even the treatment for the reaction could be dangerous. Thank God I hadn't given long-acting penicillin.

The doctor told me not to feel guilty for having given Deb the penicillin, as they had done a culture, and penicillin was the first drug of choice. But since she couldn't have that, they prescribed a different liquid antibiotic.

The first thing the doctor did, after giving her injections for the penicillin reaction and spraying something superficially on those boils, was to slice into the boils with a sharp scalpel while nurses and I held her down. Poor thing, it had to be awful. The doctor didn't sew up the place he had cut, but put in a rubber drain. We stayed in the hospital, and that night Debbie was running around, still looking swollen but obviously improving, much to the doctor's relief and surprise.

I begged him the next day to allow us to go to conference; he did, giving instructions about soaking the wound a few times a day and requesting we bring her back in immediately if there were any complications. After a couple days, it was obvious the medication wasn't working, and we had to return to the hospital. This time a fellow missionary and I held Deb down as the doctor again sliced through the flesh; the other missionary was horrified. She let the doctor know what she thought and he said, "It's just flesh. It will feel better with the pressure off." And he changed the antibiotic again. Deb got well with the antibiotic change, but she hated to go to that hospital for a long time thereafter; she detests the scar to this day.

The doctor said that had we not been in Asunción at the time Deb reacted to the penicillin, we would have lost her. He also said she would probably never pull through another penicillin reaction and to keep a medical bracelet or necklace on her. Amazing how God just happened to allow us to be going to Asunción the very day she got her first penicillin injection. *Again, how good God is to protect His own.*

Steve and Debbie

Dave and the girls

45

A FUNNY INCIDENT THAT HAD TO DO WITH DEBBIE

Several weeks before we left Tupãrenda for our first furlough, a new family moved in with us to *learn the ropes* of what was going on in the work, while we got ready to leave. They had one daughter at the time, close to the same age as Debbie.

The Periks had just received their barrels of belongings and started to sort things out. We had given them our bedroom, and we slept in the living room. One day Dee overheard Debbie and JoAnna talking in the bedroom, sitting on the bed saying, "One for you, and one for me." She went to see what they were sharing only to find they were eating the Ex-Lax that had been placed in the top of one of their barrels. The girls thought they were eating chocolate. According to the evidence later, they had eaten quite a lot.

ANOTHER COW STORY

One of the missionary couples who had lived at Lima Ty was transferred to another location and wanted to sell their cows and horses. Fred was encouraged to buy a cow by the co-worker who remained and who explained how much cheaper it would be than buying the canned powdered milk we were buying. There was only one interesting thing involved in that transaction. Fred failed to mention to me that he was buying a cow to see what *I* thought about it. I say that, because normally we talk over any big purchases, and lest you wonder why I would be so nosy as to have to know he was buying a cow, there was one good reason. As I expected, *I*, not Fred, ended up milking the cow!

And, to top it all off, he chose the cow that was hardest to milk because he was told she was much younger and would last a lot longer. Fred didn't like milking, nor did I, but I got stuck with being the *milkmaid,* as I was the one always trying to *free* Fred from as many domestic duties as possible so he could study. Is milking a *domestic* duty?

After a time, there was an epidemic of "hoof and mouth" disease among the cattle on the property, and our cow was among those that contracted it. The manager of the ranch said it needed to be treated with sour oranges. I refused to be the *veterinarian* for that little job, rubbing the cow's mouth and hooves with sour oranges. That's when I said to Fred, "I am milking that cow no longer; the calf can suck." And so it did. We never owned another cow no matter *what* co-worker thought it a good idea. Powdered milk served our family well with much less stress and frustration.

Home Schooling, Schedules, Etc.

All of our children were home-schooled whenever we lived in the interior—and even part of the time when we were in the city for lack of funds to put them in the Christian school in Asunción. We were grateful we could keep our children with us. In fact, that is one of the main reasons we chose to serve in Paraguay. The Paraguayan field didn't have a missionary kids' school—nor were we told we had to send our children away to a mission school. The field didn't have a mission school until 2006 or 2007, and since then it is by choice that some parents send their children to the mission school, which is located in the Mennonite town of Filadelfia, in the Chaco. It's a much better location than Asunción and located such that the children attending there are able to see their parents frequently. Home-schooled children, living in faraway locations, join the others at the MK school once or twice a year for special programs, all having a chance to do special things together.

Once I started home-schooling on the station, we had to slate the medical work for afternoons and evenings only—outside of emergencies. It took a while for the Indians to adjust to such a schedule. They were not *time oriented* people, and they wanted the freedom to be at our place all day long if they so desired. We had to ask the children to come play in the afternoon rather than all day long also, as it was too difficult for Steve to stay focused on his school work with other children outside playing, as he'd have liked to be out there himself.

Steve was a first-rate student, but being our first child, I required far too much of him—my expectations were much too high. We encouraged him to memorize a lot of scripture as a young child, and consequently he developed an excellent memory; and though the strong discipline benefited him in later years as far as scholastic training, I've wished I had been a more experienced teacher at the time—not totally *laid-back,* but still able to *let up* a bit.

Our children played with the Indian children in our yard or on the soccer field behind our house; they quickly picked up the language and had a better feel for it than we did in some respects. Fred was having difficulty with some of the untranslatable words in Guarani that just got thrown in here and there for *feeling*—but it was often impossible to give an accurate definition on such a word. I would always tell him, "Someday you'll get the *feel* of it. I can't explain it." And he'd say, "I'm sick of hearing I have to get the *feel* of it. I don't feel it!"

One of the words he was having difficulty with was "ra'e." One day when Steve sat down to his desk, he wiped his hand across it and said, "It's sticky ra'e," and Fred heard it. So I said, "Now do you get it?" "Finally!" My guess is that some of our kids still throw Guarani and Spanish words into their English. Some things just communicate better, seemingly, in the other language—or maybe it's that we've lost the ability to broaden our English vocabulary for lack of use. Dora once said in front of my mom, using the grammatical pattern of Guarani, "It fell from me my dolly." My mom said, "Who taught this child to speak English?" By the way, you don't drop anything in Paraguay—it fell from you. Does that indicate anything about the culture?

A CUTE PARROT STORY

The Angaite people said they never sang until we taught them to sing. When Fred's students got together they enjoyed singing songs I had translated into Guarani. Our neighbor had a parrot that always sat and listened when Fred's students were singing; he obviously learned the songs.

One day a teenage boy wanted to buy a belt at the company store, but he didn't have the money, so he sold his parrot to the Paraguayan ranch boss so he could buy the belt. The problem was that every afternoon the man and his friends gathered together after work to drink. The parrot thought it was time to sing—and proceeded to sing gospel choruses, thinking it was a gathering for a meeting. The Paraguayan man was extremely annoyed. He told the boy he no longer wanted the parrot. He said, "Give that parrot to don Federico (Fred)." Fred said, "Maybe we should train parrots."

DIFFICULT MEDICAL CASES OF THE ANGAITE AT TUPĀRENDA

We were blessed as a mission to have the Baptist Hospital in Asunción, run by Southern Baptist American missionaries. We could contact our mission headquarters by radio and ask to talk to one of the doctors in case of a real emergency—needing to know what else to do in a difficult situation.

The Baptist Hospital doctors had given a two-week course to some of our missionaries on some of the most common disease problems in the country, but there were times when something out of the ordinary surfaced, and we needed their advice. There were life-or-death emergencies in which we called for a plane flight; we who called for the plane were the ones to pay for it. Flights were expensive, but there was no other way of getting out of Tupãrenda in an emergency.

There were a couple times the Baptist doctors gave us instructions we refused to follow. The Keefes worked with us a few months while waiting to join the Ayore work that was in the initial stages of opening up. The doctor once told Linda to puncture a woman's lung from the back to drain it. Linda said she was doing nothing of the sort—and I certainly didn't know how to do it. This procedure was to be performed on Susana, the woman mentioned earlier who lived fifteen more years on her TB medications.

Another time it fell to me to follow a doctor's instructions to cut off a little girl's finger. The little girl's brother had badly mangled her finger, cutting it with a machete. It wasn't clear whether it was an accident or if he was angry at her. The finger was a mess.

The doctor said to lay her hand on a cutting board and cut the finger off where the skin was no longer covering the bone. I could *not* do it. Sorry. I cleaned it up, put the child on antibiotics, wrapped the skin as best I could around the bone, and bandaged the finger and hand. I asked the father to take her to Pinasco for medical help (three days by ox-cart).

The girl's father said he couldn't possibly make that trip; he had to go somewhere else and wouldn't be back for several weeks. He said if I showed him what to do, he would be faithful to do it and see that the bandages were changed and the wound kept clean. I sewed several little mittens to be tied over her hand and stressed how important it was that it stay clean, or she could die. He was more responsible than most fathers there would have been. He took the bandage materials, the extra mittens and medication which I put into a plastic bag, and off they went. It was weeks before they returned, but when they did, he still had her hand in one of those little mittens. The bandage was clean, and the wound completely healed. *Thanks to God again*!

*****

There were many times we just had no idea what to do. We prayed, and God answered. Where there is professional medical help available, I believe in using it. When it isn't available, one does what one can. But like we've told the indigenous people we've worked with and tried to teach to care for themselves, "God is your best resource, always. There will be times you *can't* do anything but pray." I've been in those situations, and praise God, He has answered.

But, as I made that last statement, I remember a time when I prayed the life of a girl would be saved who had been poisoned by a witchdoctor, and she *didn't* live. I cried for weeks every time I thought about Rocalia and the situation that took her life.

Rocalia had recently given birth to a baby boy; she couldn't have been more than fourteen or fifteen years old. Her brother-in-law came and asked me to help her. She had already been seriously ill the previous day, but we hadn't been told because a witchdoctor had treated her. She was seemingly poisoned. For what reason we never knew.

The brother-in-law said to me, "Don't let anyone know that I told you, but she has been treated by a witchdoctor." So I went to check on her. The witchdoctor was outside laughing; people were saying, "She's going to die; she's going to die." I just expected God to answer prayer and keep her alive. I somehow thought He would show his power and heal her—no matter what the witchdoctor had given her.

I told Fred to take care of the kids; I wasn't leaving her until I could see she would be okay. No one knew that *I* knew the man outside laughing was a witchdoctor except the brother-in-law who had told me. I asked what she had to eat or drink, and no two people gave the same answers. They finally admitted she had been given something to drink from the jungle, after I said I believed this was the work of a witchdoctor.

When I faced Rocalia's father with the fact that I knew there were witchdoctors in the village who did things like this, he denied it. Then I said, "I know there are at least five of them, and I can tell you who they are." He hung his head and admitted I was right.

I stayed fourteen hours with that girl, praying for her, unable to do a thing except to hold her head in my lap to keep her from banging it against something hard. It had been twenty-four hours since she'd been given what acted like a poison, and she was suffering terribly. I tried to give her something to help calm her as she was practically wild—and she bit my hand really hard. I didn't blame her for that; she was just beside herself and seemingly couldn't swallow properly. I talked to a medical person at the Baptist Hospital later; they felt she had probably been poisoned by something that was burning out her trachea. One of the older missionaries said he had used Epsom salts to get the poison out of someone's system when poisoned by a witchdoctor and saved the person's life, but it was done soon after the fact. Much to my sorrow and unwillingness to believe it could happen, Rocalia died. I cried for weeks afterwards, wondering *why? Why did it have to end this way?*

The baby boy was raised by his paternal grandmother. The grandmother told me she had lost many daughters to witchcraft after they had just given birth. *Why?* We weren't told the whys of many things that happened back then.

When Death Occurred

One of the things the Angaite did when someone died was to either tear down the house and move it to another location, or change the windows and doors, hoping it wouldn't be recognized as the same house by evil spirits that would return to haunt those still living in the house and kill them as well. This practice continues today with many of the Angaite people. There are believers who no longer follow this tradition because they no longer fear the evil spirits, recognizing their strength is in Christ.

Fear of the powers of the witchdoctor and evil spirits is still very real among those who are not believers. It takes time even for new believers to mature and to come to a clear understanding of their freedom in Christ. They have no problem believing there is a devil and that he's battling for their souls. But until they understand the freedom there is in Christ, there's fear of the devil and a belief that they must appease him in order to not bring trouble upon themselves or their loved ones.

While there are many heartaches working among the indigenous people, there are many joys as well, and when you see lives change because of their love for the Lord, all the hard work and hardships encountered on the way are well worth it.

Anthropologists and other educated anti-God individuals will tell you these people are happy and should be left as they are. They insist that every culture must cling to their original traditions and never allow other beliefs to affect those traditions—least of all beliefs of evangelical missionaries.

According to these anti-God people, it is the *white man* and modern civilization that is the cause of all the indigenous people's difficulties, the reason they are poor and cannot progress—talking out of both sides of their mouths at the same time. On the one hand they talk about how much better off the Indian was in the woods with his bows and arrows, wandering from place to place searching for food, being medicated by his own witchdoctors, not needing modern medications, not exposed to the diseases of outside civilization. In the next breath they accuse the government of not taking care of the Indians medically as they ought and not educating them sufficiently to be able to compete in the national society.

These anti-God people hate the evangelical missionary, who has come to give the indigenous people an option of a better life in this world and the one to come—by offering freedom from the terrible fears and stress they live under daily. They are unwilling to recognize that it is some of the Indian traditions and habits that bring the most harm to them, physically and otherwise. Surely they have a *right* to hear and to choose *the alternative*.

The ungodly media has lied about NTM missionaries for years, accusing them of genocide. They broadcast such information to a world of people out there who haven't a clue of what the real truth is, because they aren't going to go see for themselves. They don't report that the indigenous people are multiplying like never before because of better medical help, education, and so on. They don't like the fact that some have left their traditional taboos that were actually the cause of their poor health, making them more susceptible to disease and death. Least of all do the ungodly want to admit that the gospel has made a big difference in the lives of the indigenous people who have embraced it.

BEFORE VACCINATIONS, ANTIBIOTICS, HEALTH EDUCATION, AND THE GOSPEL:

Babies died from tetanus, measles, tuberculosis, pneumonia and many other diseases. Many adults died of tuberculosis before TB medications were made available to them. Children died from parasites, dysentery, malnutrition and other diseases because of improper diet, lack of cleanliness, and lack of understanding about germs and how disease is spread. Most of these people groups believe that sickness comes only from evil spirits. Without education concerning bacteria and spreading of germs, they make little or no attempt towards cleanliness—not recognizing that much of their sickness may be attributed to their own lack of sanitation.

A sick child wasn't allowed to be bathed. Trying to take down a high fever with bathing in cool water was unheard of. If the child didn't want to take medicine, you didn't force him to take it, as it would disturb his spirit. Never mind that the child would likely die without medication. If the medication didn't work with one dosage, it wasn't any good and would not continue to be given. This seemed to be a carryover from the fact that it was expected that a witchdoctor could cure a person immediately. Therefore, modern medication should do likewise. We never saw anyone get well, however, from going to a witchdoctor, though we saw people die from having gone to witchdoctors. The people went to them anyhow out of fear.

During menstruation, a woman wasn't allowed to touch the food; someone else had to cook. She wasn't to eat certain foods during that time, and she dare not work in the garden at that time of the month or the plants would not grow.

Babies weren't allowed to nurse for three days after birth, because the liquid from the mother's breast was considered to be poison. The new mother wasn't allowed to eat any solid foods for a time after giving birth—which she needed for strength to nurse her baby.

Twins were considered a curse. One was not allowed to live, as they believed it had a bad spirit. After there were believers, twins were accepted. In the past, a deformed child was not allowed to live, either—also because it was believed it had a bad spirit.

A child born after the father separated from the mother might be drowned as soon as it was born or aborted some other way prior to birth.

HUSBAND-WIFE TRADITIONS THAT CAUSED PROBLEMS

Once it was known a wife was pregnant, the husband was *not* allowed to have sexual relations with her until the baby was weaned—no longer nursing…a minimum of two years! Imagine the infidelity *that* caused! The wife didn't like it—it caused a lot of fights—but she had no recourse. One girl's parents kicked the husband out and took the daughter back because her husband wanted to have relations with her while she was still nursing. They never allowed the daughter to go back to him ever, even though she had an older child from this man; she was of an age we would have considered capable of making her own choices.

Wives remained under their parents' authority, not the husbands, if there was any problem. The parents could take the daughter away for any reason. Blood relationship was considered more important than the husband-wife relationship. There was little trust between spouses.

ANGAITE LIVING CONDITIONS

The Angaite Indian housing, overall, has basically not improved in the past forty years. These semi-nomadic people initially lived off the jungle—hunting, fishing, and doing some gardening where possible. As time went on, the jungle became smaller and smaller; as Brazilians and others bought up land, the ability to roam *wherever* became more and more difficult. The government Indian department (INDI) began to buy land for the indigenous people and place them in colonies where they would be more permanently situated. Even though there are colony setups, many of the people still roam from place to place (between colonies, ranches, or small towns) looking for work as necessary.

One of the difficulties in obtaining permanent work is that so many of them are content to work only a short time for just enough money to get by temporarily; they then take it easy until they're out of food and other necessities. There's no thought of planning for tomorrow. Even in gardening, rather than to try replanting on a continual basis, they often wait until there is nothing left in the garden to eat before they start planting again.

As elsewhere in the world, there are those who are lazy and others who are more diligent—working hard at trying to improve their living situation, while many haven't bothered at all. The sad thing is that those who are lazy want to take advantage of those who work—stealing from their gardens, begging from their relatives even when they would be capable of helping themselves more.

Everyone tends to stay poor, because no one wants anyone else to *get ahead* and progress. Those who do so are often looked down on. And the sad thing is, those who do "have" end up taking care of extended family and all kinds of relatives—ultimately hardly able to take good care of their own families because of this mentality forced upon them by their culture. If they don't give to another when asked, they will be gossiped about throughout the whole colony, often with lies; they cannot handle the gossip. Those who are constant alcoholic drinkers can't keep a job for long, so they are frequently moving, looking for just enough work to eat and maybe get a few clothes. *Their* families tend to suffer the most. They often only work a few days here and there just to get some food and then sit around until they're hungry before looking for work again. They often don't even have a tin plate or spoon for each family member—let alone a bed, chair, or table.

Another reason some lack necessary possessions is that rather than go to work, they will trade or sell items they once did have in exchange for alcohol. They may do the same for food, but we have seen this happen most when the father is alcoholic. In some cases they may have employers who pay them in alcohol, because that is what they want, rather than taking food home for the family. We have given clothing and blankets to needy families during the cold weather, only to have them sell them as soon as the weather warms up. It is difficult to help people like that.

Some who have found consistent employment do try to do better. Generally, it is the believers who provide better for their families. That is one big, obvious change the gospel has brought them. Though not all of them have consistent work either, they will try harder to have a garden to help feed the family. The difficulty with that in the Chaco is that it is practically impossible to have a garden year round; it is so dry they often lose much of it for lack of water. And even if they live close to a river or creek, to carry water by hand a long distance or up steep banks isn't easy, thus usually is not done.

This picture was taken in 2007 when we made a brief visit to Paraguay.

Everyone sleeps in the same room and usually several in the same bed, if they have a "bed." Few of the people have actual beds, even now. They sleep on boards or split palm or on a cowhide on the ground. We tried hard to get the older people with TB and arthritic problems up off the ground onto boards or something other than the damp ground, as the dampness worsened their condition.

One of the more serious health hazards of everyone sleeping in the same room is that TB is more easily spread to others in the family. Also, the sputum constantly spit on the ground retains the TB germ for as long as two years, so you can imagine what it's like to have babies crawling in that. We tried to teach them to spit into a small can or some disposable container where it's not affecting others and bury the sputum. We did see a very few people adopt the practice after years of teaching—at least at public functions. It's doubtful they followed through at home.

Cooking is done in one pot over an open fire, usually outside or in a lean-to type place attached to the other part of the house. Dogs, cats, chickens, pigs, ducks, birds, or whatever animals they own have free run through the house—which is usually just one room with a dirt floor and no running water or electricity.

The Angaite used to fish, as seen in the photo above, with a type of basket. They now use fishing poles and fishhooks, and the women fish as much as the men do now.

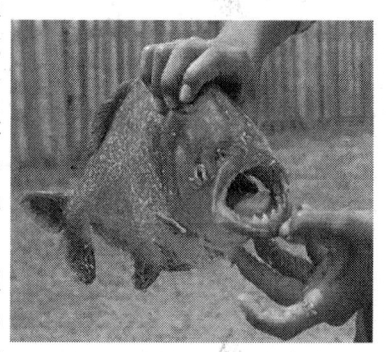

There was no way to know what kind of fish they might pull out of that basket. Can you imagine what it was like to reach in and pull out a piranha? I wonder how they coped with that problem.

We treated many piranha bites people got while bathing and fishing in the river, even after they no longer fished in this way. They still use a bow and arrow for certain kinds of fish at certain times of the day or evening.

When the river is low, there are announcements made on national radio telling the people not to bathe in the river because of the large number of piranha and the danger involved.

When cattlemen need to cross the river with a herd of cattle, they first kill a pig that will bleed in the river—down from where they want to cross—and the piranha go for that animal immediately, allowing the cattle to get across. The piranha finish off whatever they attack in short order. I refused to bathe or go swimming in that river.

⬅——— Making sure the fish is dead?

55

Every people group has a worldview that is somewhat distinctive to them, which includes their religious beliefs, taboos, superstitions, choice of lifestyle, and so on. While it is unfair to stereotype individuals—making generalities concerning the culture of a particular people group—we acknowledge that the culture in which one is raised definitely has a strong influence in the lifestyle that individual chooses to accept and to follow. Cultural cues are taught and caught at a very early age. In a society where the people do not read or write, stories, beliefs, and values have been orally passed down over the years; children grow up knowing that culture because they have lived it.

No culture is entirely good or entirely bad. Both aspects are present in every culture. The missionary does not go into an indigenous group of people with the idea of changing their culture, per se. There are aspects of the foreign culture that may be better than our own. We do not have to adopt everything of the foreign culture in order to build relationships within that culture—though it is a vital fact that we must know how to speak their language and be cognizant of their world view if we intend to share with them a message that is to be accurately understood.

The people groups with which we worked in Paraguay were *animistic*. To ignore that fact and not know how to address it would cause for *syncretism* to take place, adding on the teachings of the missionary to their traditional beliefs rather than understanding the message of the gospel as intended.

As ambassadors for the King of kings, we were concerned about presenting the King's message in a way that it would be understood by the people to whom we had gone. That is nigh impossible to do without first building a relationship with those people.

We did not have to adopt everything of the indigenous culture in order to build relationships within that culture, any more than we need to adopt the lifestyle of unbelievers in America in order to reach them with the gospel. But if we care about people as individuals, be they people within our home country or abroad, we will endeavor to build relationships/friendships through which we can one day introduce them to the Friend who is dearest to us, and who not only desires their fellowship but loves them dearly and longs for them to know Him as their personal Savior.

Where Satan has held people in bondage and fear for hundreds of years, we know we are treading on dangerous ground when we enter his territory; we're aware of the fact that there will be a spiritual battle for us and for the people whom we have gone to reach. But we believe those people have a *right* to the opportunity of hearing the gospel—a right to be released from bondage and fear under which they live daily.

We never had to teach these people about Satan and demons. They were very much aware of the fact he was alive and well, battling for their souls. They lived in constant fear of demonic powers and the consequences of witchcraft on them or their loved ones. What they didn't know was how those powers came to be, nor that there was an alternative to follow. They believed the demons were their dead relatives who had come back to torment them or to take their lives.

In teaching these people we started from the beginning with the creation story—who God is, the story of Lucifer (Satan), and the fact that the demons they feared were fallen angels who had chosen to follow Satan. God had thrown them out of heaven, along with Satan. They are not their dead relatives; it is the demons that fool them into thinking so. Once these people could read, they didn't question the truth of God's Word.

ANGAITE WORK MOVED TO NEW LOCATION

The Tupãrenda work was later moved to a place called San Carlos, near the river, where the people could have their own land rather than living on the ranch property. Those working for the ranch were welcome to remain living there, but those not working were told they had to leave. (That large ranch was later sold and went through several different owners over the years.)

The corporation that owned the ranch, at the time NTM missionaries lived there, offered the mission some land as a tax write-off for the Angaite people. The title would be handed over to the Angaite when they were ready to handle the responsibilities themselves. NTM of Paraguay paid for the expenses involved in the transferring of the land.

The missionaries oversaw the move and helped in the setting up of the colony on the "new" land. They began a cattle program to help set up an economic program for the people, along with several other trades: making bricks and charcoal, doing carpentry, cutting firewood, and so on. Things went well as long as the missionaries remained in charge, but the whole idea was to make the economy indigenous and for the people themselves to take charge when they were ready. Because they lived on the river, it would have been possible for them to sell bricks, charcoal, firewood, cattle, and whatever else they produced to boats passing by. At the time, they had no desire to personally take on that responsibility. They wanted the benefits without the headaches of the oversight.

People were sufficiently trained to oversee the work, but they wanted to have a *patrón* rather than take on the responsibility themselves. The culture embraced the idea that all the Angaite people be on equal status; no one wanted to oversee their fellow Angaites. Someone had to lead and manage things, but they wanted the missionaries to forever oversee the work and *hire* them to do the work, as was done initially. But the missionaries were being distracted from the spiritual end of the work; it was suffering in the effort to keep the economics going. Besides, it was important for the people themselves to become self-supporting. The missionaries could not be there forever.

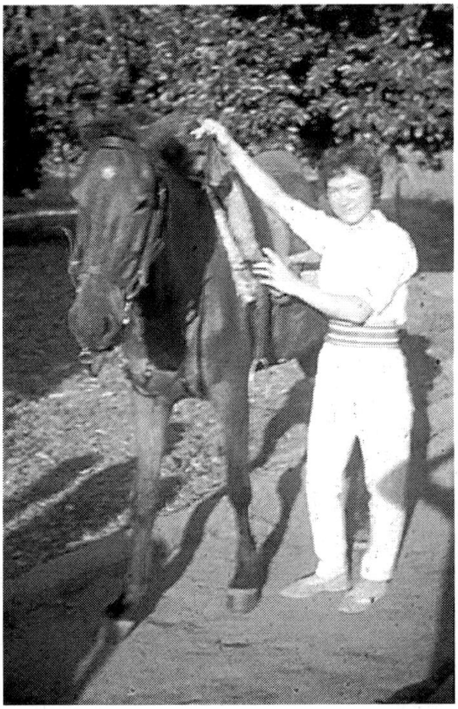

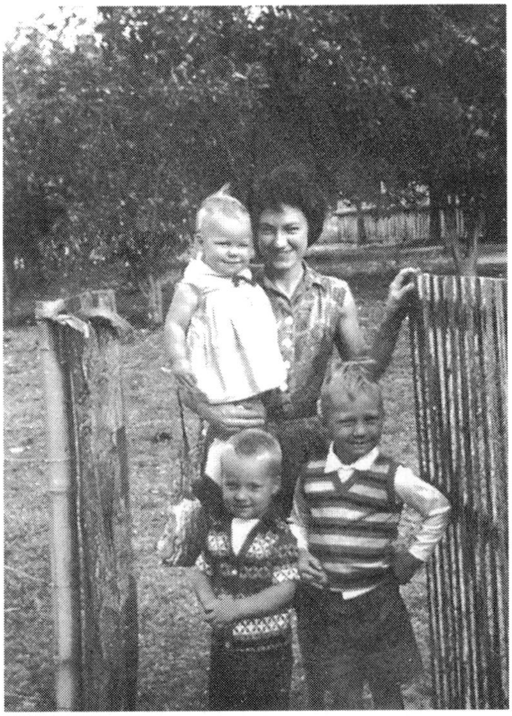

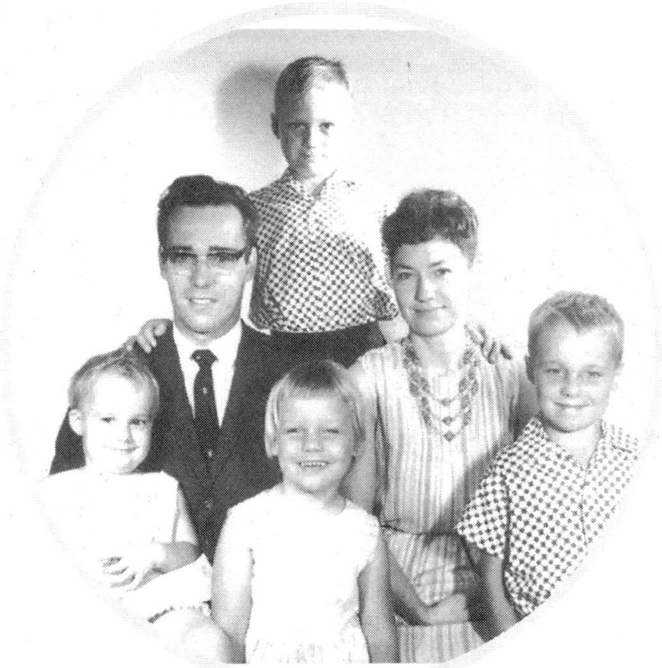

The missionaries had permission from the government to do certain things, and each year they had to give a report of what was accomplished and state how much longer they felt they would be working in that location. As time went on, the encouragement was toward indigenizing everything, as far as both the government and the mission was concerned.

The purpose of the cattle program was to provide not only meat, milk, and cheese for people in the colony, but also to be a buffer to help when the community might have a medical emergency in the future with no missionary there to help. They could sell a cow to a neighboring rancher for money to go by boat into Concepción for medical help. It would give them finances to pay for medications and treatment.

When it became obvious that a large cattle program, belonging to the colony, was not going to work (after several years of trial), cattle were offered at a very cheap price to any individual who wanted his or her own milk cow; later on they should have calves from that cow. Thus, little by little they could potentially have more animals of their own, whereby they could better care for themselves.

A few people kept their cows, but the majority sold them or ate them before very long. They never learned to plan for the future. They lived only for today. And even now the majority of them still live that way.

Our house at Tupãrenda

The young man on the right is Inocencio. The one on the left is Lucio. These two young men were some of the first to accept the Lord and some of the first men Fred discipled. Lucio has had his difficulties spiritually, but we heard recently that he is now faithfully walking with the Lord and desirous of teaching God's Word to others.

The man in the picture on the left (Basilicio—nicknamed *Brasil)* was the first man to accept the Lord. He's the one who told Fred about the witchdoctors who tried to put a curse on him. Years later a witchdoctor tried to put a curse on Basilicio, who was teaching God's word in another colony. "B's" brother-in-law told me that the witchdoctor asked *him* why it didn't work on "B." The brother-in-law told him it was because "B" had the power of God protecting him. Quite a testimony!

6
LITERACY AND THE ANGAITE TUPĂRENDA CHURCH

LITERACY

To gain the confidence of the Angaite people in Tupărenda we first began to help them with their medical needs. Before long we also started literacy classes for those who wanted to learn to read and write; we included some arithmetic because, as the people didn't know their money or correct weights and measures, they were easily cheated by the nationals in the area. Everyone wanted to join the literacy classes. We didn't know how to choose who should be the first to begin, so we allowed all who were interested to attend, and then wondered how it was going to work to have such large classes.

It didn't take long before most dropped out after they found out how much work it was going to be to learn. That made it a lot easier to teach just a few with the idea that once they could read and write, they could teach others. And Fred insisted on that. When he had taught a young man through Primer 1 and started on the second book, he told the young man, "Now I want you to teach someone else the first book."—to which the young man said, "But I can't; I don't know enough." To that Fred said, "You know Book 1, so teach Book 1." And Fred made sure he did that, following up and being there for him if he needed help. When that young man's student finished Book 1, *he* was required to teach someone else what *he* knew. It was amazing to see how it multiplied. Fred was soon teaching a class of *teachers*, then going from group to group observing them teaching others.

One young man named Inocencio was quick to learn and taught many others to read. When a young man or a child would come asking for a book of his own, Fred would ask if he could read. If he said "yes," Fred would ask who taught him. Most often it was Inocencio. It wasn't long before Fred knew that anyone taught by Inocencio did know how to read. Inocencio ended up being the first Angaite schoolteacher years later after the group moved to San Carlos. He married and had a family; years later we learned he had drowned in the river. We never knew the story behind that event, and neither did anyone else we talked to.

> These are the first young men whom Fred discipled that helped teach others to read and write. ⟶

62

Tupãrenda Church

After a few men who had been in Fred's literacy classes came to know the Lord, Fred started teaching them individually. He had one-on-one discipleship classes as well as teaching a few men together in a class.

The men Fred was teaching God's Word said, "Everyone needs to hear this." They wanted group meetings. We began meeting with the people outside. Then the people wanted to have a church building. Fred asked them if he could get permission from the ranch boss to use the carts and oxen, were they willing to work without pay. They said they were. So Fred went to get permission. The ranch boss didn't believe they would work without pay, but they did.

Everyone was excited about having their own church for the first time; when it was done they insisted on meeting *every night* for the first few months. We finally had to quit having night meetings because of the mosquitoes getting so bad and the potential for spreading malaria.

OPPORTUNITIES TO HELP NEIGHBORS

Because Fred could fix just about anything, one way or another, there were times when he was able to repair or fix something at the Big House on the ranch, as everyone called it. It was a two-story house—a beautiful home out in the middle of the Chaco, built by an Englishman some years earlier. It was where the Scottish ranch boss and his family lived.

One day I was over visiting with the boss's wife, who had become a good friend. Her husband was gone to Asunción, but he was expected to return with the British Ambassador and his wife. The pump for the cistern, which lifted water up to their house for indoor plumbing, was not working. The Paraguayan ranch mechanic tried to fix it, but he couldn't get it to work.

The wife tried to get Indians to fill the water tank by bucket; the tank was way up in the air and meant going up a ladder to fill it, but they were afraid and didn't want to do it. I happened to be there visiting when this was going on, so I said, "Maybe Fred can fix the motor." I went home and got him, and he did fix it—just in time, before the visitors arrived.

Another time he fixed a windmill for the ranch. Fred is actually nervous about heights, but he tied himself to the windmill and up he went. He tried to get Juancito (an Angaite) to go up with him, but he said, "No way; the last Indian that went up there fell and died for three days." (Unconscious for three days?) Fred managed to do the work himself, using a tractor, a couple of pulleys, and a gin pole.

The ranch boss was impressed not only with Fred's knowledge but also with his desire to be helpful. One day he said to me, "Fred is the first preacher I've ever met that knows how to work." We all know there are a good many preachers who know how to work, but evidently he hadn't met them. It was quite a compliment and a good testimony.

When I taught our children Sunday School, along with our co-worker's son, the boss's daughters attended also. We really appreciated the friendship of that family. There were several months one year when we had no co-workers; it was comforting to know that family was there. And I especially appreciated knowing they were there when Fred was gone and I was alone on the station—just me and the kids.

While we were living in Asunción (our second term), that family also moved to Asunción for work purposes for a while before transferring to Brazil. When I was sick with paratyphoid, that friend was the first to come take away all four kids for the day and tell me to just forget about the kids and get some rest. She took the kids home with her to play with her kids and fed them their meals.

Fred and I made a trip to visit this family in Brazil after not having seen them for twenty years. It was just as if we had never parted. Friends like that are rare indeed!

*One measure of our likeness to Christ is
our sensitivity to the suffering of others.*

7
Home Assignments

As necessary and important as furloughs are (now called *home assignments*), they are not without their problems and adjustments—more so for some than others. Some of us think we don't need a long "break" from our work and would like to make a quick trip to our home country just to visit family, friends, and supporters and get right back to work again. But we probably need the *change* more than we realize. While a *rest* might be in order, I found furloughs to be more stressful than restful.

Regardless of how difficult it may be, it is important to have personal contact with family, friends, and supporters, so they understand how to knowledgeably pray for the missionary family and the work they are involved in. Letters alone don't seem to do it without reconnecting from time to time in person.

Although we always enjoyed the time and opportunity to reconnect with people, constant traveling—being in a different home day after day and sometimes having every meal of the day in a different home for days on end—is hard. Not that we didn't appreciate the hospitality of all those who were so kind as to have us in their homes. And we did meet a lot of new people who were interested in missions by spending time in their homes.

There doesn't seem to be a perfect answer as to how to make the home assignment easier. Occasionally, home churches have homes or apartments specifically for their missionaries on furlough with all the household necessities provided for them so they don't have to "start from scratch" buying up things with which to live while on furlough. That is especially helpful to families who plan to stay put in one place during the school year for the sake of the school age children. But I'd say this is not typical of most cases. It never happened for us.

Although family and friends may think it a treat for the missionary family to be back in the United States, where they may (or may not) have more conveniences and less pressure than the mission field, that's not always how it is. About the time I no longer felt like a *duck out of water*, it was time to return to our work. There's no place like home, regardless of how simple it may be—and "home" now for the missionary family is what they left behind upon returning to their home country.

Not only have the missionaries changed after years of being overseas in a different culture, but it also appears that everyone in their homeland has changed. Old friends often don't bother to keep contact anymore.

Something few of us realize until after the first furlough is that things are in constant change on the mission field, too; we find changes we don't expect upon our return. Nothing remains static. You soon find that the order of the day is *flexibility* in the life of the missionary, no matter where the geographical location.

What we call adversity, God calls opportunity.

Home Assignment (1967–1968)

Our entrance back into the United States the first time had some amusing experiences—and some not so amusing. The two boys did not remember anything about the United States; they were one and two years old when we left for Paraguay. The two girls had never been here before. My brother Jim was meeting us at the Miami airport.

After getting off the plane, we were walking through the airport towards the customs' agents when Debbie spied a black person and very loudly proceeded to say, "Look, Daddy, there's a *black* man." Though our kids had lived with Indians and seemed to not even notice their color, they had never seen a black person. The man heard her, of course; he was walking right next to us. Fred responded to Debbie with, "Yes honey, and he speaks English." To which Debbie said, "He can't speak English, he's too black!" Fortunately, the man understood the situation and just smiled. Fred explained she had never been in the United States before.

None of our kids liked to travel in the small mission airplane, or in a car. They were used to the open air—horseback. We had instances when they got sick in the airplane, and if they could stay home in the Chaco rather than go to Asunción in that plane, that was always their preference when they were small. We had to travel in a car up to my brother's place in Fort Lauderdale, Florida; I never gave a thought to the fact the kids might not handle the drive well. Jim is a fast driver—so it's drive fast and stop fast—and after a little bit of that, Debbie vomited all over me, herself, and Jim's new car. I was embarrassed, to say the least. We stopped at a service station to try to clean things up a bit and were bawled out by the attendant there. I was ready to hop back on the plane for Paraguay. It was not a pleasant welcome.

After spending some time visiting family and supporters, we spent most of our first furlough at the Fredonia, Wisconsin, missionary training center. Fred taught missionary students, and I did bookkeeping and secretarial work for the staff. This was our first Christmas in the United States with all the kids. It was very different from what they were used to in Paraguay. I believe they acquired a different value system, having been raised in Paraguay where simple things were appreciated and not taken for granted.

I don't remember much about that year, but I do remember that the director of the boot camp, Jim McKnight, had cancer and was in need of a car. The staff and students all got together and bought him a used car that was in good condition and handed him the keys one day—calling a special chapel. That was fun to see; he couldn't figure out why the students were calling a special meeting that he didn't know about. What a surprise he got.

Jim didn't have the car very long before some drunk guy—who had made a bet with a friend at a bar that he could get home in short order—ran into him and made a mess of that car. Fortunately Jim was okay. The car was pretty messed up. Fred was determined that the body work could be done and the car put back into running order again. He and one of the students, who was a welder, went to a junkyard and found a car from which they cut out the fender, replacing the original fender of the wrecked car and welding it into place. I did most of the sanding on that car. Fred did the painting. A kerosene furnace was on in the garage, and what a surprise we got the next morning.

The furnace had exploded in the night, and the newly painted car was covered in soot. I think Fred just about cried, until he realized the paint had dried prior to the soot getting on it, and it was ok. Jim drove that car for a long time afterwards—even though it wasn't a perfect *fix it* job. No one had the finances to have it done professionally.

Return to Paraguay 1968

Upon our return to Paraguay, we were asked to be involved in field administration, living in Asunción. Fred was the administrator, the buyer for missionaries who lived in the interior, and he took care of the government paperwork as well, representing NTM of Paraguay to the government. I was bookkeeper and guesthouse hostess; we were responsible for radio contact three times a day, contacting each station for prayer requests and orders of supplies (food, medications, building needs, whatever). It took time to learn how to buy for each particular missionary. Some wanted substitutes when desired items weren't available, others did not. Though it may sound like an easy job, it was sometimes harder to work with missionaries than with Indians, probably because our expectations of missionaries were higher.

This type of work is considered "support" work on the field. Today it seems that church people in the United States tend to underestimate the importance of the support worker on the field. We hear people putting tremendous importance on the church planter and the Bible translator, forgetting that the support people work hard to supply for those people working on the "front lines" so to speak—so they can remain on their stations to do their work. Without support workers, the work of the interior missionary would be very difficult, particularly in tribal work. No one living in the interior at that time had personal vehicles or means to get out of their stations except by the mission airplane, which was important in emergency situations.

We had a difficult time finding a place we could afford to rent while living in Asunción and had to move a couple times during that four-year term. Every place we lived, because it was cheaper rent, needed lots of scrubbing and painting. I don't even remember how many houses I painted inside. I even have the scar below my lip to show where my teeth went through (requiring painful stitches) when a straight ladder leaning against the wall slid and fell with me, paint and all! Fred was always so busy with mission work; he was never able to help with the painting. I always wondered if I could handle another move; obviously I could.

We lived in some places where other missionaries said they would never live. One thing for sure, you have to be able to see what a place can potentially become—not what it is at the time you rent it. With hard work and lots of scrubbing, I found you can make almost any ugly place livable and homey.

Our kids were home-schooled part of this term for lack of finances to do otherwise. When the time came that I had to have a major surgery, other missionaries insisted on helping us pay for our kids to attend the Christian school, which was right there in town. Later on, while we were living in the interior, we helped someone else with their child's schooling expenses.

In those earlier years, no one had insurance or the kind of financial help they seem to have today; it was amazing how all the missionaries worked together to help one another. Sometimes it meant lots of soup and few, if any, extras; but it was wonderful fellowship, and everyone seemed to be drawn closer together through the hard times.

Cheap Rent, Yes—But...

One day the sewage started backing up...and we weren't sure what to do. We went to talk to the landlady, who said she would find someone to come take care of it. The septic tank was full and needed to be emptied. There were no modern trucks with a hose to take care of such a procedure; this stuff had to be bucketed by hand. But, where do you think the septic tank was located? We were about to find out!

The room at the front of the house, which became our master bedroom, was built right over a cistern. That cistern had been turned into a septic tank that didn't drain or seep to anywhere. The tile floor of the bedroom had to be broken up to get to the septic. On top of that, the front yard had to be all dug up to find the wall to that *cistern* and break it so there could be drainage from it. Talk about smell and an eyesore in the front yard for all the neighbors to see!

The landlady, a poor widow, had hired a couple older men who needed work to do the job, and they weren't in a hurry to get it done. Worse than that, one of the men said he needed some money up front to be able to buy some food. I said, "Finish the work, then you'll get your pay." I had a feeling it was *not* a good idea to pay him ahead of completing the work.

When Fred got home, however, from doing business downtown—he gave the man some money and said, "Now, don't you come back drunk." The guy said, "Never."

When the men returned in the afternoon to work, we were having a cup of coffee in the living room when we heard a big splash. You guessed it. The guy was drunk and fell into the sewage and wasn't a bit happy about it. Fred thought it was funny, I thought it disgusting—because we then had to wait several days before they returned to finish the work.

Dora Grace and the Bees

It was during this term, while on a picnic to the creek with a couple of other families, that Dora Grace almost drowned. The kids had gone into the creek to swim but ended up around the bend, out of sight. As there was a bunch of them together, we never gave a thought to anything happening to them. The creek didn't seem that deep.

One of the older kids came running saying, "Hurry, Dora needs help." Fred ran ahead as fast as he could go; when he got there, Dave had taken Dora over to where she could grab onto a tree branch that hung low over the water. Dora was about as big as Dave, and out of fear she about pulled him under while he was trying to save her. When Fred got there Dora's face was covered with bees, while she continued to hang on for dear life, crying.

Needless to say, Dora had nightmares for weeks after that happening. It brings tears to my eyes to this day just thinking about how that little girl suffered so from the bee stings, and how nearly she came to drowning and pulling Dave under with her.

It was also during this term, while we were working in the administration job in Asunción, that an American representative of The World Council of Churches (WCC) visited Paraguay. He was very much against evangelical missionaries working among the indigenous people and was doing everything he could to try to pile up lies against NTM to get us all kicked out of the country. The Paraguayan representative for WCC was a self-made anthropologist who was known to have been at one time a card-carrying communist. His affiliations were still questionable, and he, along with reporters from the United States and England, was continually blasting the work of NTM in South America with lies. Incredibly, people seem to believe the lies that are put out by the media—the media knowing it's unlikely anyone will or can go check things out for themselves as to what the truth really is.

Anyhow, the American WCC representative happened to be at the International airport at the same time our field director was; he walked up and spoke to him, saying something to the effect of, "We didn't get you out this time, but you'll see—we'll get you out yet." They've been trying since that time to do just that.

While this can be very upsetting to the missionary, who wonders how much longer he or she will be able to continue ministering in these situations, one soon learns to just take one day at a time and keep working. All the continual negative blasting away is to cause discouragement, hoping the missionary will give up and go home—but the opposite is true. You realize your time may be very short, and you had better be faithfully ministering while you have the opportunity and freedom to do so.

NTM has had a good relationship with key individuals in the government who know the truth and who have *gone to bat* for us over the years. I fear that is about to change, however—in that on August 15, 2008, an ex-Catholic bishop was sworn in as the new president of Paraguay—who has strong Marxist leanings and has filled his cabinet with people of the same inclination. There are many Catholic priests in South America who have been involved in what is called *liberation theology,* and they are strongly against evangelical missions. The previous Italian pope wrote an article I once read, making it clear *he* was against that particular philosophy, but it has continued to grow regardless.

My brother Paul had to leave the tribal work in Brazil because of the pressure for American missionaries to be removed; my nephews and nieces in Venezuela are in the same situation. They, along with other NTM missionaries, have been pulled out of the indigenous works—living in towns, trying to continue with teaching and Bible translation by indigenous people coming to visit *them*. They stay for a week or two at a time, helping in translation, and so on. The same has happened in other countries in which NTM works.

The missionaries in Paraguay presently have freedom to work with the indigenous groups, though there continues to be outside media trying to hinder that.

When God allows extraordinary trials, He gives extraordinary comfort.

8
1972 "Home Assignment"

We lived in the little town of Sutherland, Nebraska, for a year in a small house on the camp grounds of the little Sunday School Union church we had become acquainted with prior to going to Paraguay. (The church was located north of Ringgold, several miles away.) There was no evangelical church in Sutherland; our home church was thirty miles away, and we attended it when not on meetings elsewhere. It was a difficult time for our kids—which they never told us until after the fact. They never got a chance to make good friends anywhere, as we were at different churches constantly; the kids in their school were not friendly either, as our kids were the outsiders. Steve was in the eighth grade that year and finished as valedictorian of his class. There was no high school in the town; high schoolers had to go to North Platte or elsewhere.

Our kids were used to taking life as it came and never complained at the time. Steve told us years later that he would not recommend that kind of situation—for us or for anyone else on furlough. I wholeheartedly agree.

That furlough was difficult also because of the loss of my sister Judy, who died after surgery in February 1973, while she and her husband were also on furlough from Paraguay and living in New Jersey. She was twenty-five years old and left two young sons, ages three and five. We went out for the funeral and stayed to help sort Judy's personal things for Bob. A few weeks later, Bob brought the boys to Nebraska; they stayed with us for five weeks while he did some traveling on meetings.

All of our kids had the chicken pox and the mumps while in Nebraska that furlough, picking it up from kids in the public school.

Our *home* church had a split, with which we had nothing to do, right before the end of our furlough and dropped our support. I had been in that church since about the time I was born until leaving for missionary training. I was the first foreign missionary raised in the church. Though the church gave to the support of many others, none at that time had been kids who were raised in the church. The heartbreak of that situation wasn't the loss of financial support, it was the break in fellowship. A few individuals from the split continued to help us some, but we never again were supported by that church. It had faithfully given us $100.00 a month, one-third of our support at that time. But God is faithful to care for His servants, and He never abandoned us. We've had several faithful supporters die, yet God is alive and well, and when we lost support, He unexpectedly made it up through others without our saying a word and without others knowing we had lost supporters.

We have had people give to us on a one-time basis that met a special need when they had no idea we even had a need. God is like that. He enjoys doing the unexpected. Often it is those who have the least who give the most. That is humbling, and we are grateful to God for every cent that has been given to us; we feel responsible to be good stewards of all that we have. We know others have sacrificed to help us minister on the mission field, and we are grateful to them.

Here we are ready to fly back to Paraguay. Bob Kerr and his two young sons are seeing us off at the airport. Fred obviously was taking the picture.

Packing barrels and crates for our return to Paraguay was a big job. Fred was known to be a collector of things other people threw out, and he was teased about it, but many of those who laughed at the things he took benefited and laughed no more. We even took a small motorbike that was literally a *basket case*. It had been dismantled by a teenage kid who never got it back together. Fred sawed the frame in half, packed up all the parts, and made it fit in the crate. Once in Paraguay, he inserted a pipe between the two halves and put the bike back in operation. Putting all the pieces back together didn't happen in a hurry, but it did happen; and that little Honda 50 got lots of use.

Return to Paraguay—New Assignment
Yvypyte (the Center of the world)

When we arrived back in Paraguay for our third term, we were asked to go to the east side of Paraguay to a place called Yvypyte. Fred was asked to oversee the work and pull the team together. I was asked to do the first- through third-grade school curriculum in Guarani for our indigenous schools. The work was all done on a typewriter, cutting the text and graphics on waxed stencils. The finished product was sent to the Asunción print shop to be printed on a mimeograph machine to be copied and made into booklet form.

Getting our things moved from Asunción to Pedro Juan Caballero and from there to the Yvypyte colony was a bit of a hassle because of rain and bad roads, but everything finally managed to get there.

Dora had one leg in a cast for the first three months from a badly broken ankle acquired on a visit to another station interior prior to our move to Yvypyte. She wasn't even allowed to use crutches for the first six weeks; she was back on a horse as soon as the six weeks were over.

There was already an old military house available for us to live in, so we didn't have to do any building and were able to immediately get to work on our assignments there. The language of the indigenous people in this location was Guarani, so we didn't have to learn another language to work with them—just continued to add to our already acquired vocabulary, a never-ending task for as long as one lives in a foreign country.

Literacy and discipleship

The *Ava* people didn't live in a village like the Angaite. They were on Indian colony land, but it was extensive, and their houses were comparatively far apart from each other. It was quite a distance to go teach some of those people, so Fred and the kids involved in teaching generally went horseback or by trailbreaker. Fred taught two men who were interested in spiritual truths, and Steve and Dora taught literacy one-on-one to other individuals. It was impossible to teach the people in a group situation at the time. It has only been in recent years that the missionaries have been able to combine teaching classes for this group of people. Initially, the chiefs were strongly against their people learning to read. It was one of the slowest of NTM works in Paraguay in which to reap fruit, but it has become one of the most vibrant works today.

Some Ava houses in the area nearby Yvypyte.

This trailbreaker was a great bike for the area. It could go anywhere. Extra fuel could be put in the wheel wells—left empty, they served as flotation tanks.

*In God's service,
our greatest ability
is
our availability.*

The House Is on Fire!

One of the missionary families went on furlough and would be transferring to a different location upon their return, so a new young couple came to stay in their home to work on the station.

Julie wasn't acquainted with the potential danger of wood-burning stoves with a grass roof; she built a fire in the wood stove to bake some bread on a windy day and got the fire too hot. The house had wood walls and a grass roof, typical of many houses in the area. A teenage Indian boy was hollering something to Julie in Guarani, but she didn't understand what he was saying. Our Debbie was there and said, "The house is on fire!"

All three men were off the station, having gone to town for supplies. Three of us other women who were on the station ran to help. Steve and the Indian boy climbed on top of the house and started throwing off the grass roof, hoping to save the house, but it proved impossible because of the strong wind. I took out the kerosene tank from the refrigerator and moved it outdoors; one of the other women and I picked up that big old refrigerator and carried it outside. How we did that I will never know; the guys couldn't believe it either. We asked Julie if there was any other kerosene or gas in the house; she didn't think so.

When it was obvious we couldn't save the house, the single girl missionary got upset and wanted to open the door to the storage room, as there were things in there that belonged to another missionary family on furlough. We said, "No way, don't you dare open that door." We had no more than said that when there was an explosion from 13-kilo gas tanks that were stored in there, used for cooking on a gas stove. So one of the co-workers on furlough lost everything they had left in storage.

Afraid that the other co-worker's house was in danger, I ran down to our place and cranked on a huge diesel Deutz engine to pump water for Steve to wet down the grass roof on the other co-worker's house. How I ever turned over that engine is a miracle—strictly an answer to prayer as it had to be done by hand, and I could never do it again.

When the men came home that evening, what a shock they got. The kids met them up on the road first and told them, but they didn't believe it until they saw the house burnt to the ground. Something interesting was that as we walked around and saw all the mess later, there was a piece of paper from a tract or book, burnt all around the edges, which read, "What Meaneth All This?"

The couple who were to live in the house that burned down moved in with us with their two little girls. It was interesting with teenagers and little ones, trying to keep the bigger kids quiet while little ones napped. In addition, we didn't allow our little Pekinese dog in the house because of a baby crawling on the floor, so the dog wasn't happy with the situation.

Two days after the fire, a twister came through, and what a terrible mess! At least thirty large trees on the property fell like toothpicks, but no one was harmed.

← Dave

𝔊he cost of obedience is nothing compared to the cost of disobedience.

← Steve

On the move again

76

Fred was often out for committee meetings or other mission business for all the years we ever lived in Paraguay. Once while he was gone, Steve went to swim in the river, which was right near our house. He dove in, not knowing a jagged log had come downriver and was stuck where we normally swam. He came up white as a sheet, cut in both arms with a lot of what was supposed to be *inside* hanging *outside* from one arm. Since there was no way of getting out for medical help, and it was after the last radio contact of the day, I cleaned out the wound, put what was hanging out back in place and closed up the wound with a couple good butterfly bandages over the area. I gave him heavy penicillin shots for ten days as per the doctor's instruction by radio the next day.

Girl beat by family to rid her of evil spirits

The worst case of parasites I ever saw was that of a teenage girl who came to the clinic here for help; her whole body was swollen, her eyes almost shut, worms coming out her mouth and nose. She insisted on eating dirt. Her family, out of ignorance, was continually beating her—trying to beat out the evil spirits they thought caused the worm infestation. That's when I first learned worm-infested people crave dirt. Even grown men were known to eat dirt when badly infested with worms.

Changes in store for the Sammons family

We had been at Yvypyte almost one and a half years when we were asked if we would be willing to go to the Ache work for Fred to co-ordinate the work on the station while the previous coordinator went on furlough. I was asked to do a linguistic analysis of the Ache language, develop an alphabet and put it into writing so the Ache could learn to read and write their own language. Fred had come home from a committee meeting and told me he had told the committee we would pray about their request. He wanted to talk to me first and pray together before giving the leadership an answer. My response surprised him, probably me, too. In tears, I said, "And what's there to pray about? If we're to go, we go. But it's not what I *want* right now."

Sometimes you just know a decision is *right*, even though it's hard and not of your choosing at the time. I knew somehow that the decision was right, but that didn't make it easy.

We were happy working at Yvypyte; we had a good working relationship with our co-workers, and I didn't want to move. I don't remember now how long the family whose house burned down were living with us, but I do remember that when we were ready to move, it rained every day for about two weeks, so the road wasn't open and we couldn't go anywhere.

When we did leave, the kids and I went to Asunción first to wait for Fred. A military colonel who worked in the Indian department in Asunción insisted that Fred stay at Yvypyte long enough to oversee the building of a decent bridge over the river that crossed to the colony where we were living at the time. The previous bridge was quite precarious, to say the least. I always walked across the planks rather than ride anything over it. It was scary.

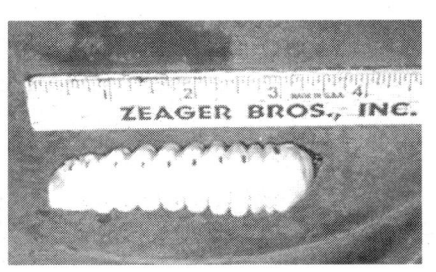

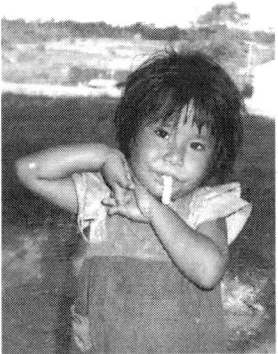

In the Ache village acquiring language material

9
Move to Cerro Morotĩ (White Mountain)—Ache village

We arrived in Cerro Morotĩ a short time before our annual field conference. Marv Cole, who was field director at the time, made it clear he wanted us to be at the conference. In that Fred was on the field committee, he was required to be at all conferences, and they wanted me there, too. I did not want to go because there was so much to do with unpacking. I knew I only had a short time to do the Ache language analysis, and I had four home-schoolers; I just wanted to get settled and started on what I had to do. You can guess who won that discussion; I went to conference.

We tried to get our things inside the house and settled into some order before leaving to go to conference. The Ache people had such crude manners that I wondered how I would ever feel comfortable among them. They were dirty, even though they lived not far from a beautiful creek that flowed from a spring.

They would wipe their noses and put it in their hair, on our screens, walls, doors, wherever. They spit on the floor, having no respect for the wood floor. They were as opposite as could be from the Angaite in their personalities. They were outgoing, emotional, boisterous, fun-loving—but able to get super angry as well, and often mean to each other. They were totally unpredictable. I wasn't sure I was going to like living in this place. They were in the windows, constantly watching us. Some would even just walk into our house without invitation any time they desired to do so.

An Indian woman would wipe her baby's bottom with her hand after it had a bowel movement, wipe it off on whatever was close by, then not wash her hand before picking up food. It was gross. I saw many unspeakable things I didn't like.

Thank God I went to conference. I don't remember who the special speaker was that year. All I know is that by the time conference was over, my heart had changed toward going to the Ache, and I was ready to work—asking God to give me a love for those people. And He did.

In March 1975 we were at last living in the Ache village—together as a family again. Right at that time, that place was a *hot spot* because of the WCC and articles they had printed and distributed internationally concerning this very work, trying to expel us from the country so that missionary work among the tribes might be discontinued. They had chosen this particular spot as their main concentration but worked on other spots simultaneously. They had their man among the Ava people in the Yvypyte area too, trying to undermine anything the missionaries did. It was at a very serious point because of rotten news media and lies being printed daily; unfortunately, people tend to believe what they hear on the news—not going to these places to check out the facts for themselves.

The true Christian is one who is right side-up in an upside-down world.

Some of the headlines (*all lies*) from various magazines and newspapers that were being circulated throughout the world—England, the United States, etc. were collected by our field director:

"MURDER, TORTURE, MANHUNTING, CULTURAL DESTRUCTION…IN THE NAME OF RELIGION AND BACKED BY OFFICIAL POLICY ATROCITIES ARE BEING CARRIED OUT IN SOUTH AMERICA! IN PARAGUAY THE GUAYAKI INDIANS ARE BEING HUNTED FROM THEIR FOREST, SOLD INTO SLAVERY OR LEFT TO DIE IN A REMOTE CAMP THAT IS BEING SUPERVISED BY AN AMERICAN MISSIONARY WHO TRIES TO ONLY 'SAVE THEIR SOULS'…TWO GUAYAKI WOMEN HELPLESS AND STARVING…UNCARING WHETHER THEY DIE OR LIVE" …

A systematic smear campaign was underway by ungodly anthropologists to rid the country of evangelical missionaries working with Indians. The Scriptures aptly say that we are in a spiritual warfare.

The Ache people (as they called themselves) were known as the Guayaki by the Paraguayans. They were a feared group of people. They hadn't been that many years out of the jungle at the time we went to work with them. The military had brought them out of the woods to this particular colony setting. The Indian department had invited the NTM missionaries to go in to work with the Ache, to help them economically, medically and educationally. They knew, of course, that we would also take the opportunity to preach the gospel to them. They really didn't care as long as we helped in these other areas, as they recognized the Ache needed help; the Indian department themselves didn't have either the finances or the personnel to do the job.

The Aches had personal gardens, but they also grew corn, soybeans, and peanuts on a larger scale for resale as a colony. Three hundred banana plants were brought in shortly after we moved there; many different things were tried to help them build a better economy.

Our kids enjoyed teaching the Indian teenagers to play ping-pong. Those people were quick to learn almost anything. Steve helped in the Indian school and studied ham radio on the side. He earned his Paraguayan Novice License while there. Dave worked in the store and was taken up with grooming and caring for a horse that belonged to a missionary on furlough. We had many things stolen by the Aches that year. Paraguayan neighbors told them what things they wanted; they would then steal for the Paraguayan and sell the item at a cost far below what the item was worth. But the day they sold their corn sheller, they got a surprise. Fred told them he wasn't replacing it. They could shell by hand as they had done before the sheller was purchased for them. They knew where it had gone; if they wanted it, they could go get it.

The Aches stole our saddles, as well as other things, and sold them to the Paraguayan neighbors. But the thing I felt the worst about being stolen was all of our kids' new school books that had just arrived—and we never did get them back. We had to reorder.

Visitors had arrived that day on the station. We had brought in store supplies and many machetes, among other things. Because the house was small, and we and the visitors filled it up, I told Fred to just leave the supplies out on the porch. "No one is going to steal them." So I thought! They stole everything, including our recently arrived school books from the United States. That included books for four students for a whole year!

The next day I went everywhere, begging them to please give back the books, but no one wanted to admit who had stolen them. I even asked them to just throw them back in our yard at night without us even having to know who did it, but the books never returned. As to the store supplies, the machetes, and so on, Fred refused to buy more for a time. When the Ache asked for more, he told them they knew where the others went; he didn't buy more for a good while.

As to the school books, we never found out until years later, after there were believers, what they did with them. They buried them out in the woods, having sold the store items to the Paraguayans. They were afraid that if they returned the books, we would know for sure they had stolen them. We knew anyway.

While we were living in the Ache village, an anthropologist from the University of Kansas showed up wanting to do a kinship analysis of the Ache people. He tried for almost a week to find someone in the village who could translate for him while he asked the information he desired. Though he was fluent in Spanish, there wasn't an Ache there who could speak Spanish.

Missionaries, on the whole, haven't been too happy to see the anthropologists come into the Indian villages, as they often cause more trouble than not. They say they will give back the information they have received so it can benefit the people, but generally that is not the case. The Indians themselves are leery of them because they are strangers; they don't understand why they ask all the questions they ask.

After the anthropologist couldn't get anyone to help him, I asked our missionary team if they would allow me to do so. That way at least we would know what he was about and what kind of information he was after. They agreed I could work with him.

Dora (fourteen years old) took over the cooking in our house, and everyone did what they could to allow me to work with the anthropologist. It turned out to be a benefit to the people, because working on the kinship analysis I was able to also have the information needed to help those people get birth certificates while we were still in the village with them.

There wasn't anything the Aches wouldn't eat as far as animals were concerned, whether dogs, cats, rats, monkey, coati, or whatever. A favorite was grub worms. It was in the Ache village that we learned to eat donkey meat. It turned out to be better than any beef we could buy in the area.

Whenever an Ache woman was giving birth and crying out or groaning with pain, there was always a group of women around who *encouraged* her with such negative comments as, "It's because you were bad to your husband," or some other negative thing she had done that caused her to now have all the pain. But as soon as the baby was born, all was happiness and everyone forgot all the bad comments that had been made.

The same was true when we took care of snakebite victims. There would always be a group of people around to say that it happened because the victim had done bad things to someone else or some such thing. They usually carried on in front of the person about how they were going to die. It was a practice that I absolutely detested. Once the person was well, all the bad things said were seemingly forgotten.

These people were some of the most loving people I had ever met. At the same time they were capable of being the meanest. They delighted at the thought of tying an unfaithful woman up to a tree and beating her. Once while we were living there, the husband of an unfaithful wife caught her and shaved off all her hair, took away her clothes and left her to walk back through the village naked.

Because the Aches were nomadic they were used to just leaving their mess behind them; so when they settled into a village situation, they tended to let the mess pile up around them. They would have mandioca (yucca) peelings, sweet potato peelings, and "who knows what" all over their houses and yards. We would try to get them to realize it was healthier to clean things up. They would usually clean things up when asked; somehow it never occurred to them to do so otherwise.

LIFE IN THE JUNGLE

There are so many more things that could be shared about the Ache people, but it would take up far too much space. They are a very interesting people. They had suffered a lot while living in the jungle; once they were out, they did not care to return.

Because they were nomadic and on the move all the time, it was difficult for the elderly to keep up with the others. Their stories say they often had to leave the elderly behind to die in the jungle alone. I won't bother to repeat some of the descriptive details that would gross you out. But life for them in the woods was not all so glorious as the anthropologists would have you to think.

The Ayore people—a group with which my sister Alice works—also had to leave many of their elderly people in the woods as they traveled; but rather than leave them to the wild animals, they buried them alive at the person's request. They also buried many babies alive, nursing their dogs instead as they continued to travel through the woods. They said it was too difficult to live in the woods, constantly moving, with babies.

Years later many of those Ayore women cried, after coming to know the Lord, mentioning how sorry they were for having buried so many of their children. No, those who think it is good to leave the Indians alone because they are happy as they are, are very mistaken.

Thank God for the Help of Our Kids

Not long after we were in the Ache village, one of the families went on furlough, leaving us with one less family to help in the work. There went the guy who did the medical work and helped with physical work on the station. Shortly after that, another family was called to return to the States, because the wife's father was dying. There went the schoolteacher and the backup medical person.

That left two of us families to do everything. Often, Fred wasn't even on the station because he was Field Coordinator and traveled to help at the other stations at least two weeks out of the month; sometimes it was longer. The other man on the station kept the economical part of the work going with the Ache people.

I was working on the language analysis and school materials; we ended up with sixteen primers, using material I had gathered from their own stories I had on tape. Steve, Dora, and Deb helped do the teaching. Deb was very young, so she was helping beginners. When Fred was present he oversaw the teaching and taught as well. Dave took over the work in the colony store along with some young Ache men. The kids worked willingly and kept up their school work at the same time. It was heavy for them that year.

The medical work fell to me; I had Steve and Dora helping me as needed. Dora was fourteen years old; Steve was sixteen. They were a big help.

Because of my working on the language and our kids in home-schooling, we asked the Ache people not to come for medical help in the mornings unless it was an emergency. There were some older people present in the village, however, who had more recently come out of the jungle, and they did not understand anything about schedules. If we failed to take care of them when they came, they would probably just take off for the woods angry and not get the help they needed. So, every morning I had Steve and Dora make the rounds through the village before they started their school work, to see if there were any older sick people who needed attention right away.

The emergencies always seemed to happen when Fred was gone. Thankfully, the other co-worker was one whom I could call on for help any time, and he graciously came to the rescue to help in an emergency. We had a few snakebites, and there were always fights among the people where they cracked open heads and gave each other all kinds of wounds. The way husbands and wives treated each other was terrible. One day I was saying how badly a wife looked as I treated her wounds, and someone said, "If you think she looks bad, you should see her husband!"

Not what we have but what we use, not what we see but what we choose –
These are the things that mar and bless the sum of human happiness.

While living in the Ache village, Fred helped setup a sawmill with a band saw purchased from some Mennonites to cut boards for the Ache to have wooden houses. The Ache had to personally make the cedar shakes for their roofs.

A water system was also set up with a pump in the creek which worked automatically from the water pressure that came from a spring, thus pumping water up into the village for our use as well as for the Aches.

Debbie helping beginners in the Ache school

Dave working in the store

Steve teaching Math to young Ache men Some of these young men were already married.

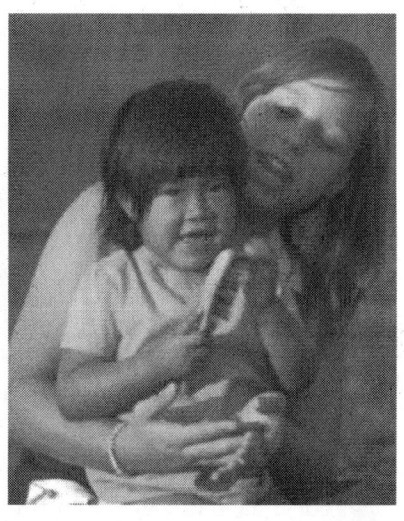

Dora helping someone with schoolwork

Steve on ham radio, having earned his Paraguayan radio license

BAD NEWS

One day someone came to say a woman was hurt, but the person didn't act like it was any emergency, so I said to Dora, "Go open the clinic." I told the people to take the woman to the clinic right away, and I would follow. Then I looked out the window and saw that the woman's blood was spurting out of her wrist like a donkey's blood when the Indians slit its throat. Her husband had slit her wrist with a razor blade. She said it was because she couldn't find his spoon, and he accused her of stealing it. But others said it was because she was either unfaithful or flirting with another man.

I ran outdoors immediately, asked some guys to please pick her up and carry her to my house, and then sent one of the kids quickly for Paul (the other co-worker) to come help. That was a scary situation. Fred was gone, of course. We got the blood stopped, immobilized her wrist, *butterflied* and bandaged it and put her to bed. She lived close by our house, so we took broth and soup to her several times a day, giving her heavy doses of penicillin daily. After a week she wanted no more injections and ran off to the woods. She came back a month later with the wound beautifully healed. That was only an answer to prayer.

THE POWER OF FEAR

Another time I was called to go take care of a teenage girl at night who had fainted. It was dark; the girl had gone out to go to the bathroom, something frightened her, and she passed out. When she came to, she said evil spirits had scared her. She asked me if I was afraid of them. I said no, because I had a greater power protecting me.

I went home that night so desirous of being able to soon tell them the truth of the gospel in a way they could understand. They lived under such bondage. They believed that all good Ache went to the sun after death, and that when they died, a good Ache who was already at the sun would come back to mediate for them and accompany them back to the sun. Bad Aches turned into jaguars, who came back to try to kill their own people.

They believed that any Ache who was killed by a jaguar in the woods, would in turn become a jaguar himself and come back to kill others of his family. For that reason, if a man *were* killed by a jaguar, I was told they left that man's family out in the woods alone to be killed by the jaguar, so he wouldn't bother the rest of them. They had many harsh ways in which they treated orphans. If it was taboo to do something they wanted done, send an orphan to do it. If the orphan was killed, so what? That was their thinking.

They were frightened by the falling stars, certain that it was an angry relative coming to burn them up. They would run inside and hide. They did the same when they saw a rainbow, saying it was a big snake wanting to swallow them up. The Angaites previously believed the rainbow was a snake, too. Interesting how Satan has turned something wonderful that God has created into a lie that brings fear to those who believe it.

When there were storms they would wail and cry, believing it was their relatives who had gone on before—up there causing the storm, urinating on them. They saw we weren't afraid of any of these things and started listening to things we had to say about God and His creation. We told them the story of the rainbow. They had a story about the flood, too; it was very different, of course. We told them about the advantage of having things written down in a book so the story would stay *straight* and not be changed by each one who told it. We told them about God's book.

These people were very open about their beliefs; and they were not shy at all about telling the things that happened in the past, as were some other groups who had been out of the jungle for many years. We found the Angaites to be very closed about their beliefs and prone to cover them up. They had evidently been made fun of in the past by the nationals. For many years the Angaites refused to teach outsiders their language. Even after there were believers, it was very difficult for the Angaites to talk about the past beliefs, taboos, and superstitions the people held, but the Aches had no such inhibitions.

Mediator?

When an Ache woman was pregnant, men would bring her meat to eat from their hunting trips; the child was named at birth with the name of the animal of which meat she had eaten the most. There was a particular uncle who was to tie and cut the umbilical cord of that baby, and an aunt who was the first to hold it. Those persons had an emotional tie to that child for life. They were responsible to see that the child got to the sun at death. This person would return to get the child and mediate for him or her in arriving to the sun.

We heard of cases where a baby was buried alive with the individual to whom it had that tie, so that the person would be satisfied and not return to take someone else. One of the young men I worked with as a language helper said he was put in the grave with someone who had died when he was young, but someone pulled him back out before it was too late.

I had a story that one of the Aches had given me on tape that mentioned an old woman coming back (from the sun) to take an unworthy man that had died. She said to him, "You keep your mouth shut, I'll do the talking." She mediated for him because he wasn't worthy to get there on his own merits. I used that analogy to explain the gospel of Jesus Christ to the men I worked with. It was a good comparison of the fact that because we weren't worthy of going into God's presence ourselves, we needed a mediator, Jesus Christ.

There weren't any believers yet when we had to leave the village; we were only there on a temporary basis to cover for others on furlough. The missionaries were still learning the language, and I was assigned to develop a Pedagogical Grammar for them whereby they could learn the language more quickly. I worked on that project for three years, completing it in Asunción after we left the village.

10
MOVING AGAIN

Before we left the Ache village we knew we were in for a move, as the previous coordinator was returning from furlough; but we weren't yet sure to where we were moving. Dave had made it known he would certainly rather live in the city than in the country. Our kids had no American peers their own age much of the time we lived in the interior—and they were missing that, because the Ache their ages were either married already or doing things in which our kids could not participate as believers.

We told Dave we would pray about his desires, and that either the Lord provide us with sufficient funds to allow him to go to boarding school in Brazil, or maybe even transfer us to the city. His response was that he did not want his desires to affect our serving where we felt God wanted us to be.

Then one day Fred called a family business meeting. "We have something to discuss," he said, "and we want your input." Their response was: "Where are we moving to now, and what do *we* have to say about it?" Fred told them it was important to us that they be informed as part of the family and have input on the decision that needed to be made.

Dave spoke up and said, "Why is it always *our* family that is asked to move all over? Why doesn't someone else move for a change?" The truth was that our particular gifts affected our moves.

Fred, wanting to have a little fun with the kids said, "We've been asked to go to Bahía Negra." "Bahía Negra?" (said one of the kids—probably Dave.) Bahía Negra was the most remote station in the Chaco where NTM worked. Fred waited to see the reaction. After a bit, Dave said: "Well, if we're going to Bahía Negra, let's get going." Then Fred told the kids, "We're not going to Bahía Negra, but we are praying about where God *does* want us to go."

As it turned out, we were asked to go to Asunción. That was an answer to prayer for our kids, who appreciated the opportunity to be with kids their age for a change. No one even knew we were praying about the school situation Dave had mentioned.

An interesting note here about Bahía Negra: when John and Deb came to Paraguay as missionaries many years later, there was a need for co-workers at Bahía Negra. Before Deb ever saw the place, she said, "I'm anxious to see this place that people consider *Siberia*." After living there she said, "God sure knew where best we could serve. I'm happy to be serving in Bahía Negra. It's definitely the right place for us." It's interesting to see how God prepares our hearts for the place HE desires us to serve.

When it came time to leave the Ache village, I sat out on a log in the woods and cried. I had come to love those people, and I so much wanted to be able to do the Bible translation for them, but we were asked to move when the missionary on furlough returned. My prayer was that someone else do that translation if I could not.

THE FIRST ACHE BELIEVERS

We were moved to Asunción to work on the leadership team. Fred was involved in traveling, and I was still working on language lessons for the Ache missionaries.

One of the Ache men became very ill and was taken to Asunción for medical help. We took him to the Baptist Hospital, but some visiting anthropologist—who didn't like evangelicals—complained to the Indian department that the sick man belonged in the military hospital, under the Indian department's care, not ours, and not at the Baptist Hospital.

When we took him to the Indian department for them to place him in the military hospital, there was no room for him, so we took him home to our house until they had room for him. He was in that military hospital for five months. I was there to visit him every day during that five months, with the exception of a very few days because of other responsibilities, in which case I sent someone in my place. The young man's name was Santiago. He was twenty-two years old, married with a couple of children. He had three surgeries during those five months. He had a very rare disease they had never before seen in Paraguay. They actually removed tumors from his chest that weighed several kilos three different times over the five-month period.

One day in November when I went to see Santiago, known to be one of the strongest men in the Ache village, I prayed that he would be outside alone where I could talk to him about the Lord. I had no idea at that time that he was not going to live through this ordeal.

I arrived at the hospital grounds, and there he was outside waiting for me to come. I prayed for an opportunity to explain the gospel clearly to Santiago; as far as I know, he accepted the Lord that day. He said he wanted to accept the Lord and prayed with me.

It was my hope that Santiago would be the one to go home and tell the others, but as it turned out, God had other plans. He never went home again; he died there in the hospital. It was with the third operation that he bled internally and died; the 11 lb. tumor that the doctor removed from his chest had been attached to all vital organs, and when the doctor scraped to remove the tumor, the wall of his chest was left like a sponge seeping blood.

I was there at the time, as I had stayed with him even through the night when he had his surgeries. A family member or friend was expected to be there to take care of the bedpan, etc. He was in a room with about thirty other men, no screens, many mosquitoes and it was hot and humid. I was standing with a hand-made Indian fan, fanning him to keep the mosquitoes off and trying to keep him comfortable from the heat. Occasionally I stopped because it was so tiring, and he'd say, "Ruthie, fan me." I finally said, "Put the sheet over your head for a bit."

Santiago's blood pressure was dropping fast; I asked the nurse and doctor on call to please call the surgeon. It was about 10:30 p.m. The surgeon came and opened him back up; he then told me about the internal bleeding and that Santiago was gone. That doctor had been a Navy doctor and was on staff at the Baptist Hospital. Santiago probably couldn't have had a better surgeon, but it was so hard to understand *why* it had to end this way.

The interesting thing that happened, however, is that because of Santiago's death, many of his people got concerned about life after death, as they had been hearing the message of the gospel from the missionaries. Paul found one of the young men (who had helped me with language work) out on a log crying one day. He stopped and asked him what was wrong. Fausto said, "If I should die, I don't think I would go to heaven." He accepted the Lord right then, as did several others shortly thereafter.

A bit later Fausto was brought to town sick, scared to death that he had what Santiago had. He stayed with us; we took him to the hospital for x-rays, etc. It turned out he had a bad case of hookworm which was treatable. I asked him to make me a tape after he got back home in his own language about his trip to town. What fun I had listening to that tape and his explanation of the things he had seen in town.

Buses were *containers that let off gas*; he felt like he was flying behind Fred on the motorbike when Fred took him to the hospital for tests. He had some interesting descriptions of the instruments and equipment used at the hospital which I don't remember anymore. He felt like the bedroom he was in at our house was like a "cave" (brick walls). He had never seen television before and wondered how those people got inside that machine.

Later on, Fausto was the first to share God's Word among his own people. He was also the first indigenous Ache schoolteacher in the colony.

LIFE BACK IN ASUNCION

It was in July 1976 that we moved to Asunción. Dave, Dora, and Debbie attended the Asunción Christian Academy; Steve studied at home, continuing his schooling by correspondence. He was a big help to me as Fred was traveling the field as Field Coordinator and was only home two weeks out of the month. I continued working on the Ache analysis and language lessons for the other missionaries still working in the Ache village. Everything was done by typewriter in those days—much more time-consuming than if we had owned computers.

It was during this time in Asunción that Fred and I were asked to represent the field of Paraguay at a New Tribes Mission Leaders' Regional Conference in Manaus, Brazil, for all of NTM's South American work. Fred was there to discuss field- and government-related business; I was there to represent the language areas and future planning.

Fred and I were fortunate to have gifts that complemented each other; wherever we were placed, we found plenty for each of us to do in the area of our specific gifts. We were thankful to be able to have our children with us in our missionary ministry. We always felt our children were our God-given responsibility; we knew our years with them and our opportunity to have input in their lives would pass by quickly. It happened faster than we imagined. We could never have accomplished as much as we did had it not been for the help that our kids were to us and to the work in which we were involved.

During Steve's last year at home, because he was young and almost finished with his high school correspondence courses, he was able to spend some time in the interior helping out on another station where they needed help.

In April 1977, Steve returned to the United States to attend college, staying the first few months with Fred's sister and husband. I missed him like crazy. He was like my right arm—always there if I needed him as Fred was still traveling constantly. The first few weeks he was gone I continued to set the table as if he were there, and when I'd say, "Where's Steve?" the others would say, "You know where Steve is." And the tears would come again. He was only seventeen years old. *How did we ever do that?* I now wonder. I don't think we would do it again.

After a few months of living with his aunt and uncle, Steve moved out on his own, but it was not easy for him. He had to pay all his own expenses; we were not in a position to help him financially. At least he knew how to *rough it*. I'm not sure how long it was he slept on the floor without a bed or other furniture, but it was a long time.

Dora had her fifteenth birthday in June 1977, in Asunción. The fifteenth birthday was a very special one for all Paraguayan girls, and her algebra teacher asked if we were going to have a birthday party for her. Many of Dora's school friends had extravagant parties for their fifteenth birthday; there was no way we could afford to do that. Jan Brown, Dora's algebra teacher, said she would like to make Dora's cake as a gift; she felt we could have a nice party that wouldn't cost much at all.

We did have a party for her (the only birthday party she ever had), and it was a fun time. Her teachers from ACA came, as did some of the NTM missionaries in Asunción at the time, as well as many of the high school students from ACA.

The cake was gorgeous with a wishing well on it. It looked like a beautiful wedding cake. The Paraguayan tradition is to place little charms into the cake with thin satin ribbons attached that hang from the cake. Before the cake is cut all single girls at the party each take hold of a ribbon and pull at the same time to see which one gets the "ring." Only one ring has been inserted into the cake. The one to get the ring is the first to get married, they say.

On the left is the algebra teacher working on the cake.
On the right are the teacher and Dora at the party.

Negative Outside Publicity

At this time there was a lot of pressure from outside publicity against missionary work. Satan was busy trying to keep the indigenous people from getting the gospel; our letters were always asking for prayer and encouragement for those working among the indigenous people. The anthropologists and ecologists talk about "freedom" for the Indian—by which they mean going back to stone-age type living; they have no idea what the Indians want—nor do they seem to care.

Two books were published in England in 1977 against the work of NTM with the Ache people. The authors had spent all of three hours in the village one day; it was unbelievable the lies they were able to dream up after such a short visit. In one case pictures were taken of another Ache village that was connected to a non-evangelical group and attributed to us; the pictures of the colony in which we worked, which had decent housing, a water supply, and so on, was attributed to the other group. Not only did these discrepancies show up in printed articles and books, they were posted on the wall in the Indian department office; and when Fred saw it and made mention of the error, it was just shrugged off and nothing was done about it.

Fred was in charge of handling the government paper work at this time. Permission was given to bring in missionaries for one more year. Clearance had to be gotten one year at a time. God has kept the doors open to Paraguay in spite of all the opposition of ungodly organizations trying to close them.

Sometime during the three years we were in Asunción during this term, Fred became the field chairman. There was a lot of responsibility to the field chairman's job back then; mission personnel in Asunción was kept to a bare minimum so that as many missionaries as possible could be sent to the interior to work in the tribal areas. Fred was confronted constantly by having to respond to the lies of the opposition—going to government offices at their request, getting phone calls from England and being put under pressure to answer questions on TV when he didn't even know that TV reporters were going to be present.

House Hunting Again!

Asunción was an expensive place for us to live on our income; each time we lived there we ended up having to house hunt extensively to find something we could afford to rent. We had only been a little over a year in the house where Dora had her fifteenth birthday when we had to find another place to rent because the bank was foreclosing on the owner of the place we were in. We finally did find a place, but it didn't have a telephone, and we never were able to get one the whole time we lived there. Cell phones didn't exist back then.

We talked to Steve by ham radio (November 1977) and learned that he had totaled his car in an accident because of icy roads, but he was unhurt. Interestingly enough, it was the same day I felt constrained to pray especially for him, feeling something was wrong but not knowing *why* he needed special prayer. God is so faithful!

It's hard having your kids so far away—knowing they, too, are hurting and often don't find a *home away from home* where they can go when they need to talk to someone. We had no idea the adjustment it would be coming back into this culture until we came back to stay on a more permanent basis ourselves.

The pressures of missionary work are very real. Satan is busy doing his best to curb spiritual interest and growth within the Indian works by causing problems from within and without. We were so short-handed personnel-wise that we were constantly before the Lord re-evaluating our priorities, defining our objectives in light of our personnel, jealously guarding our time of daily communion with our Lord and giving of our time and strength first to the spiritual areas of the work. We found that economic involvement can be a hindrance rather than a help, if it takes the place of the spiritual because of personnel shortage. We tried hard to keep it in its proper place. That's not easy when surrounded by so many needs with such a shortage of personnel to carry on the work. True, the people needed help economically, but they also needed the Word of God. While it often seemed there was no solution in sight, we were thankful to be serving the God of the impossible and continued to pray for more workers.

More Negative Publicity

In April 1978, we mentioned the following to supporters, asking for prayer: A man from Temple University of Philadelphia, Pennsylvania, wrote a book called "Genocide in Paraguay." He had gathered various articles other people had written and compiled them into his book. The book stirred up so much commotion that this man was invited by the Paraguayan government to see for himself that what he had written was untrue. Instead of being honest, he twisted the facts and passed on barefaced lies.

These lies were passed on to newspapers outside the country that played up the atrocities of the missionaries. His three final conclusions were as follows: (1) for the American government to give more American money to an Indian organization in Paraguay who is teaching the people to stand up for their rights. A few months ago, one of their leaders was kicked off a large cattle ranch for his Communist activities, yet these are the kind of people this man wants the U.S. taxpayer to support. (2) His second conclusion was to kick New Tribes Mission out of the country. (3) The third was to topple the present government.

That same month our house was broken into in the night while we were sleeping. Thankfully, our kids were all at a camp for the weekend. A Paraguayan friend said it was good we didn't wake up until the two men who had broken into the house were back outside again, or they would probably have killed us. They had been through all the rooms in the house. They had taken the girls' purses, containing their Paraguayan identification cards—difficult to replace. There was nothing valuable in the purses except those cards. While they got away with some things, there was a lot more on the porch they intended to take—the motorbike included.

Fred woke up hearing his name in his sleep—thinking I had called him; then he heard whispers, got up to see what was going on and hollered at me in Guarani to get the gun; and they got scared and ran. I thought Fred was having a bad dream. We didn't even *own* a gun.

Fortunately, the electric typewriter was in the shop for some repair, or it would have been taken, as it normally sat on the desk right in front of the window they crawled in through. It was returned from the shop the very next day. The thieves stole our keys, so all the locks at the NTM office had to be changed. They obviously knew where Fred worked, as they circled the NTM grounds a couple nights, but the police dogs and the caretaker scared them off.

In May 1978, I was asked to make a trip to Manaus, Brazil, for a conference on Bible translation and literacy materials, representing the field of Paraguay. I met another couple in Bolivia and traveled on to Manaus with them. Dora took over the cooking and household duties at home while I was gone.

We were due for furlough in June 1978, but due to the shortage of personnel, we were asked to stay an extra year—making that term a six-year term.

In August 1978, Debbie went to Vianapolis, Brazil, to the NTM boarding school for her eighth-grade year, wanting to learn Portuguese. Other missionary kids from Paraguay were there, and she wanted to join them. Fred had received some money from his aunt, who had recently died; it was just enough to cover Deb's expenses in Brazil. One reason we let her go was that we had always been against boarding schools, but being in leadership and never having experienced such, we thought it might be good for us to find out what it was like.

How we missed Deb's lively spirit at home with us! She got homesick, but she completed the year and said she felt she learned a lot from the experience. She did learn to speak Portuguese. We really didn't change our minds about boarding schools for us personally, but one thing for sure we do know—if you decide to send your children away to a boarding school, you support the school and encourage the child to finish what they started. Mid-year, Deb would have stayed home at the Christmas break had we let her. But we had told her before she went that if she made the decision to go, she would have to finish out the year—which she did.

Both Dave and Dora finished high school early that term. Dave asked to return to the United States to live with Steve. So in November 1978, he was packed, ready and anxious to spread his wings. He planned to get a job and live with Steve to help him with the rent. But in January 1979, Dave enrolled in the New Tribes Bible Institute in Waukesha, Wisconsin.

In March 1979, Dora, having graduated early, left for Waukesha to help my sister Bev—at Bev's request, because Bev was expecting twins shortly and had four other young children (all under school age) and couldn't afford to pay for help. Both our boys were in Waukesha; they felt it would be okay for Dora to go as we would be returning there ourselves in May 1979. Were we to do it over again, we would probably keep the kids with us until we could return with them. It was not an easy transition for any of them.

11

HOME ASSIGNMENT—NEW TRIBES BIBLE INSTITUTE

When we got back to the States in May 1979, we sat down with our kids to discuss what we were going to do about housing. The Bible School wanted Fred to teach, but they didn't have housing for us as a family. Our kids had already told us there was no way we could afford to rent—so just go live on the NTBI campus without them and they'd *go it on their own*. No way! We felt we should be together as a family, so we talked more with the kids about it, prayed about it—and found out, they too, preferred to be together. It was true that our finances were such that it was impossible for us to rent a place in Waukesha on our NTM income. No one wanted to rent to us when they heard what our income was.

It was the boys who came up with the idea of helping us with the rent so we could be together. Steve was working, and Dave had begun working. They said they would be glad to help pay the rent, along with us so we could live together as a family; so that's what we did for one year. We had difficulty, even then, finding someone who would accept us on that basis, but finally someone decided to give us a try; the rent was faithfully paid each month, of course. We knew it would be—one way or another, but it was hard to convince landlords of that.

LIVING AT NEW TRIBES BIBLE INSTITUTE—WAUKESHA

After one year of furlough, we were asked to continue at NTBI on staff and live on campus. Fred would continue teaching and I would work as bookkeeper in the finance office.

During the summer of 1980, Fred was gone most of the time, leading a *Summit Team* to Paraguay (short-term mission trip) to do some building at the Ayore station.

Later on, the NTBI leadership asked us to stay on longer than we had previously planned, as frequent personnel change was hard on the school, so we told the Paraguayan Field leadership to carry on without plans for our return. This gave time for us to be there while the kids were in transition as well. Deb was still in high school, but the others were all college age.

When it was decided we would stay on at NTBI, we joined the Waukesha Bible Church, working on various committees, helping in Awana, and making many new friends.

There were adjustments living at NTBI with college-age kids, but we all lived through it. While our kids were in the midst of making lifetime decisions, so were the NTBI students. We had students in our home daily, wanting to talk. Some were struggling; we cried with them, prayed with them, and made lifetime friends with some of those students who are today serving the Lord in hard places—still keeping in touch, faithful to what God has called them to do.

I started taking some college courses by extension at this time, specifically subjects that would be helpful in our ministry in Paraguay. It was the beginning of a long, slow process for lack of finances and time. I also studied Morse code and acquired my Extra Class Ham Radio license so I could help missionary kids at NTBI contact their parents overseas.

Another Change in Our Lives

In 1983 we were asked by the NTM executive committee of our Sanford, Florida, headquarters to return to Paraguay to join the leadership staff there again.

Steve was attending Christian Heritage College in El Cajon, California. Dave and Tammy (having met at NTBI) had married in August 1982, after Dave had graduated from NTBI. Steve talked them into going out to San Diego County to live, where he could help Dave find work. Dora married Jim Wood (MK from Paraguay) in May 1983. She had previously graduated from NTBI and LPN nurses' training at WCTI in Waukesha.

Deb was finishing her first year at NTBI, engaged to John Van Allen. As Deb and John were planning to marry in December 1983 after John's graduation from NTBI, the mission gave us permission to wait until after the kids were married to return to Paraguay.

Once we knew we would be returning to Paraguay, we started giving things away and packing things we wanted to take that we didn't need to use at the time—knowing we would be traveling for several weeks visiting supporters before leaving. We also had Deb's wedding to think about, which was to take place just a few weeks before we left again for Paraguay.

Frequently on my mind during that time was a song I like very much, but at the same time difficult to sing as I thought of leaving all our kids behind—and knowing we were being asked to be traveling consultants upon our return to Paraguay when my first choice would have been something other than constant travel. Here's what I wrote in my journal on June 9, 1983:

> *I pray for wisdom and grace to function as God would have me function in the situation. I'm sure it won't be easy on the flesh, as my natural tendency is to desire a home to stay put in, not traveling constantly. But again, God knows what He has ahead for us, and I know He will give grace to perform what He asks of us. May I be sensitive to what God has for me without His having to put me flat on my back before I look up or learn what He's wanting of me.*

Whatever It Takes

There's a voice calling me from an old rugged tree, And it whispers "Draw closer to me.
Leave this world far behind, there are new heights to climb And a new life in Me you will find."

Chorus:
For whatever it takes to draw closer to you, Lord, That's what I'll be willing to do.
And whatever it takes to be more like You, That's what I'll be willing to do.
I'll trade sunshine for rain, comfort for pain, That's what I'll be willing to do,
For whatever it takes for my will to break, That's what I'll be willing to do.

Take the dearest thing to me, if that's how it must be, To draw me closer to You.
Let the disappointments come, lonely days without the sun, If through sorrow more like you I become.

Take my houses and lands, all my dreams and my plans, For I'm placing my whole life in your hands,
And if you call me today to a land far away, Lord, I'll go and your will obey.

Fred was excited about returning to Paraguay; part of me was, but the other part felt *torn*. It had taken me a long time to feel I belonged back in the United States; I had been ready to return to Paraguay long before we did. But when the opportunity came and I faced the realization of leaving all my kids behind—that was hard!

Deb and John were married December 17, 1983, the day after John's Bible School graduation. We left for Paraguay three weeks later. Deb saw us off at the airport and the last thing she said to me was, "How does it feel, Mom, to be going back without any kids?" That did it. I cried the whole way to Paraguay and for the first two weeks after we got there!

I had always said missionary life wasn't a sacrifice; we felt blessed to be used of the Lord on the mission field, but when we had to start parting with our kids—I have to admit, it hurt.

One of the hardest things in our later years of missionary life was not being able to be there for our kids when special events took place in their lives. For those who remained in the United States, we hardly knew their children, nor did the grandchildren really know us. It's difficult to *bond* long distance. We prayed for our kids and grandkids daily; we tried to correspond frequently and remember their special days, but we couldn't be present in person. As a result, we didn't have the opportunity to build an intimate relationship with some of the grandkids from the time they were young and watch them grow up. This was one of the main consequences to the choice we made to minister abroad. But when all is said and done, I believe today they would all say they were supportive of what we were doing, so that others might hear the gospel and have God's Word in their language.

Steve graduated from Christian Heritage College in 1984, marrying Monica Riffe in June of 1984. I had hoped Steve and Monica could be married before we left the States; they had dated for two years, but it was decided that Steve finish school first. When they did get married, Fred came back for the wedding; financially there was no way both of us could come. I missed so many special events in Steve's life; I felt terrible about it. I tried to make up for it somewhat several years later when he graduated from Bethel Seminary and was recognized as Senior Pastor of the church where he is presently ministering. I arrived without his knowing I was coming until I was already there. That was fun to do. Tammy is the only one who knew I was coming as she had to meet me at the airport. Fred had come alone earlier, so none of the kids expected me except Tammy, and she kept our secret. (Fred was on crutches, unable to drive, from a motorbike accident in Paraguay prior to his trip to the United States.)

Steve is presently the Pastor of the Lake Murray Community Church in La Mesa, California. He still takes mission trips to Brazil when possible, teaching in a seminary there. He has earned a Master of Arts degree in Theological Studies from Bethel Seminary, a Master of Divinity degree from Southern California Seminary, and recently completed his doctoral thesis for Gordon Conwell Theological Seminary.

Psalms 147:3: *He heals the broken in heart, and binds up their wounds.*

Here, from my journal on December 31, 1983, is a poem I related to from *Daily Bread*:

THE DESERT PLACE

Did He set you aside when the fields were ripe and the workers seemed too few?
Did He set you aside and give someone else the task you so longed to do?
Did He set you aside when the purple grapes hung low in the autumn's sun?
And did hands not your own just gather them in, the trophies you'd almost won?
Did He set you aside on a couch of pain, There where all you could do was pray?
And then when you whispered, "Oh, please let me go," was His answer always, "Stay"?
Did He set you aside with no plan at all, with no reason that you could see,
While your heart cried out, "In this limited space, Lord, how can I work for Thee?"
Did He set you aside with a heavy cross, And was your heart filled with despair?
Did you think He had gone and left you alone, Then suddenly He was there?
And there in the shadows, the world all shut out, Just kneeling alone at His feet,
Did you learn the answers (though not all yet)? Say, weren't His reasons sweet?

25 years married
Silver Anniversary

12
BACK IN PARAGUAY

Fred was asked by the executive committee to help in the overall leadership of the field, working in Asunción part of the time, but also traveling to the interior to encourage the missionaries and recognize the needs in each location. I set up the language program in Asunción for new missionaries as well as doing the same for missionaries living in the interior, traveling to consult in the areas of language and linguistics, to give help where needed and to encourage progress in those areas. We were there to encourage and help the missionaries.

It worked out well for Fred and me to travel as a team, visiting the stations. He coordinated along with being *Mr. Fix-it* for things that needed fixed on the station that no one else had time to do. He repaired motors, helped build, or whatever else needed done.

Because we would be doing consultant traveling, it made sense for us to live in an apartment on the mission guesthouse property. We were temporarily living in a guest apartment until an additional upstairs apartment was finished for us. There were almost always people in the guesthouse—some on "break" or in town for government paperwork, sickness, or whatever, which meant people were wanting to visit constantly. This meant getting up very early to have time in devotions and the study of God's Word before others were up and around.

We found we had to adjust again to the water and heat in Paraguay. We were again made aware of the need of firm commitment to the job God had called us to—plain old hard work in the midst of heat, personnel conflicts, lack of privacy, and so on. It was my constant prayer that God help us to *praise* and rejoice in Him regardless of difficult circumstances.

Talking over problems of the work with missionaries on the stations was often more tiring than doing hard physical work. But that is why we were there—to see how we could encourage and be of help. One has to look to the Lord for wisdom as to how to respond to the various problems and needs. There is sometimes friction between co-workers, friction between Indians and missionaries, or between Indian leaders. Everyone tends to think their ideas or opinions are the correct ones. What joy it is to see these problems resolved so the work can go ahead as it ought. One thing is for sure: God cannot bless disunity in the ranks. When people realize they are aiding the enemy by holding onto their grudges or grievances, they are generally quick to ask forgiveness and let go of them. How we prayed for wisdom to know how to show love and encouragement to all concerned. Our hearts went out in compassion to those struggling with difficult issues.

It was our prayer that God give us grace and love that would overflow toward our fellow missionaries, regardless of the problems. I recognized my need to learn to talk more to the Lord, talk less to the missionaries and *listen* more to them. And I prayed the Lord would give Fred the needed wisdom when it was time to talk and me the grace to keep quiet.

Our means of travel to the interior depended upon which station we were visiting. It might be by motorbike, bus, mission plane, or by boat. Our first trip two weeks after returning to Paraguay was a thirty-six-hour boat trip upriver. Although such a long boat trip can be very uncomfortable, depending on the time of year, it also allows for time to read and meditate, *if there* is a room available in which to rest. It's not like the *Love Boat*, believe me.

In hot or stormy weather traveling by boat is not so pleasant. We have had to sit out on the deck before in the hot sun and wind; so when there is a room available (tiny as it may be), we're happy to have it. You must overlook the lack of cleanliness and get over the fact that cockroaches are sharing your room. You never get used to them being there; it's just a fact that they will be there. In which case, if I forgot to take along a sheet or blanket, I would buy a newspaper to place on the dirty mattress. Fred always laughed at me, but it made me feel there was less chance of my acquiring something I didn't need or want to acquire. The bathrooms were something else to behold; I usually didn't drink enough when traveling, because I didn't want to visit the dreadful bathroom any more than necessary. Some people even showered in there—the room not being more than a meter square, if that, and a filthy floor on top of it.

I checked the missionaries' language progress and helped set up their study programs to work on weak grammatical areas, insisting they get so many hours a day of exposure out in the village with the people. Relationships with the people were of utmost importance. One could be fluent in the language and not have a good relationship with the people and fail to have a ministry among them, because they are only going to listen to the person in whom they have confidence. The saying is so true, that *"people don't care how much you know until they know how much you care."* Though the indigenous people may not be able to understand your language, they pick up on attitudes quickly and recognize the difference between the *professional* worker and the one who treats them as friends and equals.

It was difficult for some of the young mothers who were home-schooling to spend a lot of time in study, so we worked out a reasonable program for them, memorizing everyday phrases needed for the particular ministry involvement they had on their station. Usually everyone had some specific involvement with the indigenous people, as there wasn't enough personnel to go around without the wives being involved also. Of course, the more social one is, the quicker one generally learns the language. The indigenous people weren't looking for grammatical correctness, they were looking for friendship. They considered some of those who made the most grammatical errors to be the most fluent, because they were friendly and social. *Actions speak louder than words* holds true in any culture.

Fred was always prepared to have a time of prayer and sharing with the missionaries as a team, encouraging them from God's Word as we would all meet together at the convenience of the team. Sometimes we were on a station as long as two weeks, other times only a few days, depending on the situation and the need at the time.

Apart from giving language checks to those individuals studying language, I spent time checking over analytical problems of those individuals working on linguistics with the goal of later doing Bible translation. It was my responsibility to ask questions that would help them know what direction to go next when they were stuck and encourage them to make a decision, rather than spend weeks floundering over the same grammatical problem. Until some decision was made, it was difficult to progress. If a decision were incorrect, it would show up as one got more material from which to compare and analyze more thoroughly.

It was always good to get back to Asunción after a trip and find our mail—especially anxious to receive letters from our kids. It would take a bit of time to get back *in gear* after being gone for two weeks to the interior.

Fred was gone again for a week immediately after returning to Asunción from that first trip to another location with the field committee; I was missing him like crazy. I was still trying to *find my place* again after having been in the United States at NTBI for an extended period of time. A lot of changes take place in just a few years, and one doesn't just step in where one left off. It's almost like starting all over again with a new team, new responsibilities, new policies. I'm not saying change is bad—just that it takes time to adjust to the changes. I saw so many things I didn't understand, yet I didn't want to be critical. I was being asked to help people with things for which someone else had the "title" but who didn't have the experience—and I was a bit fearful of treading in where maybe I didn't belong. I asked the Lord for grace and wisdom to know how to function in such situations. I decided I could certainly help and encourage those *asking* me for help. There were some who needed it and didn't want it. That was another problem. I did a lot of work in the print shop when in Asunción.

There were times when I felt the need to cry out in prayer, as did David in Psalms 51:10, "*Create in me a clean heart, O God; and renew a right spirit within me.*" Psalms 51:15, "*O Lord, open thou my lips; and my mouth shall show forth they praise.*" 51:17: "*The sacrifices of God are a broken spirit; a broken and a contrite heart, O God, Thou wilt not despise.*"

I copied several verses out of Ecclesiastes that I had previously marked which I felt I was in need of reviewing. I read an article by Dr. Charles Stanley, titled "The Key to Balanced Living." He said, "Would you be willing to have someone pray for you, that you would prosper in your finances and in your health only as you prosper spiritually, and only in proportion to your spiritual growth?" *That* is a challenging thought!

My attention was drawn to the scripture's emphasis on wisdom and understanding— also the power and strength that we have in Christ—all of this being operable in my life as I allow the Holy Spirit to work through me, recognizing what I truly have in Christ according to His Word and acting upon it, knowing the *facts* are true and nothing depends upon my *feelings*.

Thank God, He *is* faithful to work out the needy areas of our lives. There is so much more joy in doing things *His way*! There is always more joy in obedience! Much less frustration if we *submit* to what He's trying to teach us. Why are we sometimes slow to learn that?

We were never in Asunción long before it was time to make another trip. Sometimes we traveled together; other times we traveled apart, depending on the situation. Fred often was on trips with the field committee, apart from the trips we made together. I was sometimes on a station doing linguistic work for weeks at a time, while Fred had to be in Asunción taking care of other field business. Those separations weren't easy for either of us.

The thing I found hardest when traveling to the interior was not being able to have light in the early morning—to be able to have devotions before there would be interruptions making it difficult to have time alone with the Lord. This was specifically true if we were in someone else's home rather than in a guest facility or a house where the owner was on furlough. In such a case, if it was still dark when we woke up, Fred would often put on a tape so we could listen to Scripture in Spanish until we could see to read—using headsets, of course, if others were still sleeping in the house.

I learned to take candles with me when I traveled. Even though it wasn't the best lighting, it was better than nothing. Fred finally found a clever way to hang his flashlight with a piece of shiny tin behind it to get better lighting for himself when he traveled alone. One way or another, you learn to *make do*. The old saying "where there's a will, there's a way" is so often true.

I don't remember where I came across this poem, but I copied it into my journal on April 2, 1984. It's about a kite that wanted its freedom from the string to fly off and do what it wanted, but when it tugged free and got its freedom, it crashed to the ground. The last verse says:

> My heart replied, "O Lord, I see
> How much this kite resembles me!
> Forgetful that by Thee I stand,
> Impatient of thy ruling hand;
> How oft I've wished to break the lines
> Thy wisdom for my lot assigns.
> How oft indulged a vain desire,
> For something more or something higher.
> And but for grace and love divine,
> A fall thus dreadful had been mine."

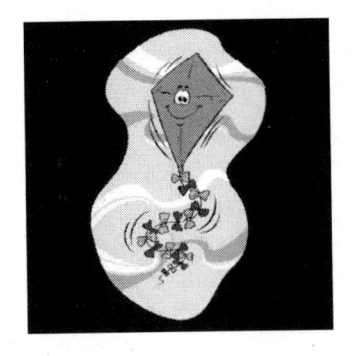

If I shirk today's tasks, I increase tomorrow's burdens.
Don't try to bear tomorrow's burdens with today's grace.

I found it exhausting to be in someone else's house consistently. Each time we returned from a trip, I would spend the next few days writing up language evaluations on each missionary checked; I would then send each of them a copy of the evaluation and a copy to the field committee. That was time-consuming, along with trying to catch up on correspondence. We always appreciated getting letters from friends and family—always hoping to hear from our kids.

There were times I felt like I was being stretched in every direction—seeing others in need of encouragement and having a hard time physically and emotionally myself. I was challenged in reading *The Training of the Twelve*. Jesus certainly portrayed a life of excellence, patience and stability. He was never in a *hurried, scurried* frame of mind, though there were times He sought rest, and He was weary. His life was in balance—He was always even tempered.

In reading *The Training of the Twelve* again, I was also impressed with how *balanced* the teaching of our Lord is. There are *negatives*, but there are also the counter-balancing *positives*. In His teaching on discipline in the church, it is obvious that all is to take place from a heart of love. Love will not gloat in dealing with another's sins, but will *hurt with* and seek to *restore*. But love also *won't overlook* sin, failing to take the responsibility of dealing with it. Balance—balance—balance. How hard it is to find perfect balance in our daily lives.

HARD CHOICES

Dora called various times from the States wanting me to be there for the birth of her first baby. I don't know if she was crying at her end, but I was sure crying at mine. I wanted to be there in the worst way—and there was no way I could go. Her baby was due toward the end of June. Steve and Monica were to be married the sixteenth of June. Steve had phoned, wanting me to go with his dad for the wedding, as we had decided that since we couldn't afford for both of us to go, Fred should go. But having just returned to the field, we had a lot of expenses still not taken care of and had to borrow money for Fred's ticket. We still didn't have our things out of customs and had no idea what that was going to cost. We had to start from *scratch* again as far as acquiring furniture and setting up housekeeping. It was a difficult time financially.

Daniel James Wood, our first grandchild, was born June 27, 1984, to Jim and Dora. Fred was able to see Dora and the baby right after Danny was born. He went from attending Steve and Monica's wedding to then going to see Jim and Dora—and he almost didn't get to stay to see the baby because of his flight schedule. That baby barely got there before Fred had to leave.

I felt so torn up inside, wanting to be there for my kids, afraid they'd not understand or forgive me for not going. But how do you go with no money? It was hard. That's all I can say, it was very hard! Today many missionaries are able to attend special events of their loved ones even though far away—by way of help from supporters, friends, or relatives, or other available finances. I'm glad for them.

*****

On August 20, 1984, we got a notice that Pam Griffis, my sister-in-law, had died in Venezuela the previous day—leaving four young children; no details. Life is so uncertain. It's a good thing the Lord knows the future, all the *whys*. He can turn to good what today seems so difficult, though I'm not sure we will always understand the *why* of some things on this earth—as I think also of my Dad's early death at age thirty-seven and my sister Judy's death at age twenty-five.

*****

It is difficult to describe all the activities and responsibilities we participated in on the field during those years in Asunción. When on the stations for consultant work, we tried to fit in and help in areas other than our *specified jobs*, as such, when there was time for that—working on whatever else the missionaries might need help with. It might be refinishing furniture, painting, sewing, mending—whatever needed to be done to help remove some pressure and give them more time to do what they were there to do. Usually, projects that had to do with motors, electricity, or computers, were saved for Fred's visits. He's a *jack of all trades,* master of none, and enjoys working with his hands as well as teaching. He always spent time sharing from the Word as we traveled together on the stations.

When we were in Asunción, people came to us, wanting to talk over various areas of their work; some needed help on particular projects—language study, literacy, help with printing their letters—numerous things. It meant setting aside our own projects, temporarily at least, to be available to others needing help or sometimes just needing to talk with someone.

It was much easier for me to be grateful for my strict mother, who was a strong, consistent disciplinarian, once I was on the mission field. The training I received at home growing up certainly helped me to be focused and disciplined on the field. It would have been very difficult to handle the responsibilities I was given to do had it been otherwise.

SEPTEMBER 23, 1984, JOURNAL NOTE:

> I went alone to Spanish church today. Fred is gone again on a field committee trip. The thought came to me this a.m.: Every day I set up a tentative work schedule, and at the end of the day I review it to see what actually *was* accomplished, to see where the *leaks* are. Why don't I do that concerning my spiritual attitudes at the end of the day? Did I walk under the control of the Holy Spirit, and were His fruits evident in my life, or were there some *leaks* I need to recognize and deal with?
>
> Do I consider, as I lay out tentative work areas, what the Lord would have me do? Am I open to interruptions He might bring? Is it really my desire to *follow* Him, to be led by Him, or do I have my own ideas about what I want to do and how I want to do it?

*****

The years 1985 and 1986 were just more of the same—constant traveling for consultant work, Fred traveling with the field committee, work in Asunción for both of us between trips—occasionally attending meetings that had to do with the Indian department and the indigenous work. Fred constantly had the pressure of answering outside false accusations against the mission. The hatred toward evangelical missions by those in England and the United States was continually present and growing.

While many of those who hated Christians and evangelicals, in particular, would say there is no God, they were sure fighting hard against Him. I could never figure out why anyone would fight so hard against someone who didn't exist, if they really believed what they said they believed. Somehow they must know deep down that the truth is otherwise.

I continued to work many hours on literacy primers for various stations, as well as working in the print shop on other projects. I did secretarial work for Fred that had to do with government business and kept up our own correspondence. It was in 1985 that I seriously got involved with the linguistic analysis of the Angaite language. That was on top of other responsibilities, because the missionary who would be translating asked for my help, as did the South American representative for NTM who had the oversight of the linguistics and translation work in South America. He was stationed in Bolivia, and he himself had completed two New Testament translations in two different languages. He came to Paraguay to better train us in translation principles, giving us the opportunity to observe him in "on the job checking" and training us to do likewise.

Neither Fred nor I had a chance to get bored, that's for sure. But even with all the work and travel, there were times of loneliness—missing family, specifically our kids. It was exceptionally hard when it meant weeks of separation for us as a couple. There were times I had to be in the interior working on the linguistics of Angaite, but Fred's schedule didn't allow him to be free to go with me. Other times he would go with me and stay briefly, then leave me, sometimes to return later to get me, and sometimes I had to travel back to Asunción by myself. It was the same later on when I became a translation checker. However, we learned to work with the situation, and we generally were able to have radio contact on a consistent basis which helped.

*****

On August 8, 1985, our second grandchild, Janelle Marie Sammons, was born to Steve and Monica. Monica's mother and Steve were able to be with Monica during the birth.

*****

On December 9, 1985, Fred's dad passed away during surgery for a heart problem; they found he also had stomach cancer. Fred left the next day to go to the United States for his dad's funeral to be with his mom and sister. He returned to Asunción on December 31.

*****

On March 28, 1986, our third grandchild, Heather Dawn, was born in Missouri to John and Debbie Van Allen while they were in language school.

Unable to be with Deb, we sent money to help on the hospital bill and paid Dora's ticket from Pennsylvania to go spend some time helping Deb after the fact. John's parents were missionaries in Colombia and weren't able to return to the United States for special times in their kids' lives either. In fact, no one on John's side of the family was able to attend his wedding. Not only did most of us lack finances to do such, but younger missionaries today may be surprised to know that it was generally not looked well upon back then by supporters and home churches for their missionaries to return to their home country for weddings, funerals, births of grandchildren, and so forth.

We knew a case where a person did return for a funeral for a parent and lost support from a church. I was unable to attend either of my stepdads' funerals, missed several weddings of siblings, births of grandchildren, and even Steve's wedding. That's how it was then.

SOME CHALLENGING THOUGHTS FROM APRIL 1986 JOURNAL NOTES:

From *Walking with God*, by Phillip Keller: "Refuse to let reverses, frustrations, discouragements, or seeming disasters distract your attention from God's will for you. Pursue His purposes. Set your sights on His loftiest ideals and aspirations for you. Let nothing intrude between Him and you."

*****

In *High Call High Privilege*, Gail MacDonald makes an interesting analogy concerning drought—speaking of Fall when the leaves are off the trees (gaining strength for blossoming Spring!), and the *down times* and seeming *dry* times in our lives. One cannot be producing fruit *all* the time, but in its season…and the dry, quiet times are necessary for regaining of strength for the future blossoming and bearing of fruit.

*****

On August 11, 1986, I wrote:
My heart goes out to some of our missionaries in the interior desiring to serve but easily discouraged and lacking somewhat in personal motivation to keep enthusiastic in the midst of trials. It's hot, buggy, and the very people you try so hard to help are sometimes ungrateful and unappreciative.

Speaking of people being unappreciative, one of the more difficult things in leadership is probably the fact that criticism often comes with the territory. It can also be very lonely. One must learn to leave things in the hands of the Lord and try to not take things personally. Although that's easy to say, it's not always easy to do. Fred always says, "God keeps the books." And that should be enough.

Lord, keep me calm, though loud and rude
The sounds my ear may greet,
Calm in temptation's solitude
And problems that I meet.

There are a couple of quotes from *Ordering Your Private World*, by Gordon MacDonald that I find challenging.

In Chapter 5 (Living as a called person), mention is made of the fact that we are only stewards of what God has given us—be it career, gifts, health, etc. He then says, "Are these things owned, or merely managed in the name of the One who gave them? Driven people consider them owned; called people do not. When driven people lose those things, it is a major crisis. When called people lose them, nothing has changed. The private world remains the same, perhaps even stronger…those whose private worlds are in disarray tend to get their identities confused."

He also says, "To order my life according to the expectation of myself and others; and to value myself according to the opinion of others; these can play havoc with my inner world. But to operate on the basis of God's call is to enjoy a great deal of order within." Stimulating thoughts!

13

MOVING FROM THE APARTMENT TO A HOUSE

In October 1986, we moved into a house that belonged to NTM. Though making the move was a bigger job than we had anticipated, it felt good to be in a house again where we would have more quiet time for study and devotions. We were still available to the missionaries who came from the interior, inviting them to our home to visit and for meals. We were on the same bus line as the mission guesthouse and within walking distance of it.

*****

One day I decided to reread *High Call High Privilege*, by Gail MacDonald, and chapter 2 starts out with, "*The bow that is always bent will soon cease to shoot straight.*" Gail brings out in her book that the need to *disengage* from the crowds so we will be more useful to people is often misunderstood and criticized. Yet without it, we are no good to anyone. That is so true. There will always be criticism, so one needs to be most concerned with what the Lord would have one do. It doesn't take long to find out in leadership that you cannot please everyone. Your emphasis has to be on pleasing the Lord and trusting Him to guide you with a gracious spirit toward all those with whom you relate.

*****

David Joel Wood was born on October 23, 1986, to Jim and Dora. On December 13, 1986, we went to the airport to meet Jim and Dora and their two little boys, Daniel and David Joel. How special it was to have some of our kids join the Paraguayan team as fellow co-workers. Being in a house with room for guests would prove to be extremely helpful later on in emergency situations when we could help with our own grandkids.

*****

In February, I had the opportunity of taking care of baby David Joel a few days while Fred, Jim, and Dora (with Daniel) made a trip out to the Ache village to check things out, as it looked like they might be joining the Ache work. Little David was a darling!

*****

On April 26, we went to the airport to meet John, Deb, and Heather Van Allen. How very special it was to have more of our kids here on the field with us. How grateful we were to be in a house where they could be with us while looking for a place to rent.

At "Nana's" house: Danny, David Joel, and Jonathan Wood; and Heather Dawn Van Allen

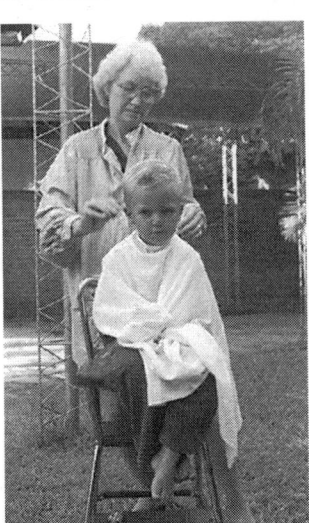

In April 1987. I came across an article Fred had copied from somewhere, reminding us it's always too soon to quit:

"It is not the critic who counts: not the man who points out how the strong man stumbled or where the doer of deeds could have done them better. The credit belongs to the man who is actually in the arena; whose face is marred by dust and sweat and blood; who strives valiantly; who errs, and comes short again and again, because there is no effort without error and shortcoming; who does actually try to do the deed; who knows that great enthusiasm, the great devotion and spends himself in a worthy cause; who, at the worst, if he fails, at least fails while daring greatly. Far better it is to dare mighty things, to win glorious triumphs even though checkered by failure, than to rank with those poor spirits who neither enjoy nor suffer much because they live in the gray twilight that knows neither victory nor defeat."
(Theodore Roosevelt, April 10, 1899)

*****

In September 1987, Jim, Dora, and the boys moved to Cerro Morotĩ to join the Ache work. We were glad to be able to go with them and help them get set up.

*****

In October 1987, I started re-reading *Hand Me Another Brick*, by Charles Swindoll on Nehemiah. I was encouraged from chapter 1 with the challenge to evaluate, rebuild and persevere. Don't give up! The enemy was working so hard against our mission work among the indigenous people here in Paraguay. It was encouraging to see how Nehemiah kept going through what seemed impossible circumstances, and to remember that when God gives a vision of His will to be done and calls us to do it, He will also empower us accordingly.

From page 73 of the previously mentioned book: "We who would seek God's best for our lives must learn to keep our eyes open and our attitudes positive—not lacking in discernment, but positive. And we must never forget there will always, *always* be opposition from those who are, by nature, negative and critical. But the work must go on. Progress should not stop because a few are critical of the plan. Remember that! [Nehemiah] did two significant things in response to the criticism: He prayed and he persisted."

I returned to San Carlos to work on the Angaite language analysis every chance I got. Sometimes Fred could be with me for a few days and sometimes not. I liked it when he could come back to get me; it was no fun to return home alone when it had to be by boat.

Short Home Assignment: February 6–August 11, 1988

We left Asuncion for a short *home assignment* in the United States. We spent the first two months in Sanford, Florida, and in California with our kids; then we started traveling to visit relatives, friends, and supporters elsewhere throughout the United States. It seemed strange for Dad Sammons to not be with Mom. I hadn't been to his funeral, so the reality of his not being present hit me as we arrived in Sanford and I again realized he was gone. He was such a special person, and I missed him.

In June we attended the NTM Refresher Course in Camdenton, Missouri. In July we traveled around Nebraska, then went on to Colorado, attending a niece's wedding and a family reunion in Denver, Colorado, on August 6. It was good to have our sons, their wives, and granddaughter Janelle there. It was hard to say goodbye to them, knowing it would be a long time before seeing them again. Fred was sick while in Denver in the midst of packing to return to Paraguay, so it was not a pleasant time for him; later it wasn't pleasant for those left behind either, as they evidently all came down with the same flu.

Though the five-and-a-half month break from our work in Asunción wasn't exactly restful, it was a change. And sometimes change is as good as a rest. In any case we were glad to be heading back to Paraguay again. We arrived in Asunción around midnight on August 12, 1988. It felt good to be home.

Dora working in the clinic in the Ache
village in Cerro Morotĩ

14
BACK IN ASUNCION

On August 27, 1988, Jonathan Dale Wood was born by Caesarean section. In the afternoon we took the other kids up to see their mom. She was weak and pale but smiling, happy with another beautiful boy.

*****

In reading John 21:21–22, I had the following thoughts: When the Lord told Peter what he was to do and what was to become of him, his question was, "And what about him (John)?" The Lord's answer was, "And what's that to you? (You) follow me!"

It's so easy to get our eyes on other people and wonder why the Lord allows them certain privileges, or doesn't see fit to allow them to suffer or go through the difficult times we may experience. Yet we aren't to question what God has for us or for anyone else. We are to follow Him completely, knowing His way is perfect. He will bring blessing out of the difficulties.

In October 1988, we made a trip out to Cerro Morotĩ, taking supplies to the station in the mission van. It was hard to see Dora exhausted and under so much pressure. Some of her own kids were sick, she herself wasn't feeling well, and she was so busy taking care of the Indians she hardly had time to take care of her own children. The Aches were very demanding, having no compassion for Dora's situation. I felt sorry for those young parents in that hectic atmosphere and felt badly leaving them in that situation. I prayed the Lord would give them wisdom to control what they could and should, and grace to accept the rest. It was a difficult place to work.

I'm again reminded that all things that come into our lives are allowed by God and can be turned to good. (Romans 8:28). As I thought even of Jim and Dora in that difficult situation at C.M., I realized God was desiring to mold them, build character into them, use them for His glory; and the very things they needed to learn maybe could best be learned through this kind of situation. Their natural tendency was to be "soft"—unable to say "no." Now they had to learn to handle such demanding situations and say "no"—or be unable to work there. We prayed that God would give them wisdom and balance in those areas.

From page 94 of *Gentle Persuasion,* by Joseph C. Aldrich: "The Bible calls us clay pots which contain a treasure. The treasure, of course, is Christ. Life style evangelism is not an attempt to decorate and shine the pot; folks need to see the treasure, not the container. Only a broken container lets the radiance of the treasure penetrate the darkness. In our brokenness we're called to be redemptive people. Sheep are most powerful when they're aware of their absolute vulnerability. If Christ (not our position, power and possessions) is lifted up, He will draw all men unto Himself."

Courage isn't having the strength to go on – it's going on when you don't have the strength.

Debbie **Dora**

The entire Wood family

John and Deb Van Allen (Heather and Jessica) at Bahía Negra—with Fred

114

John and Deb by this time were living in Bahía Negra working with the Chamacoco people. A radio message said Heather Dawn was very sick with dysentery; special medicine was shipped to them. A couple months later Deb came to Asunción on an emergency flight; a nurse on their station thought she might have a tubular pregnancy. Though it turned out that the pregnancy was normal, she had some kind of inflammation for which they put her on antibiotics. In the meantime she had lab tests done on Heather Dawn, who kept having dysentery problems.

John was on the station wanting his wife home. Because of bad weather, Deb couldn't get a return flight home as planned. If the weather was good in Asunción, it was bad in Bahía Negra. Twice she and Heather went to the airport only to find out there would be no flight. Then the unexpected happened, which would delay her from getting home for weeks.

*****

February 1989: "Takeover" of the Paraguayan Government

From my Journal notes:

February 2nd: Deb had hoped to get on a flight today with our mission pilot, but the person who had contacted him to fly that direction canceled. [Our pilots did a certain amount of *outside* flying to help subsidize the cost to our missionaries. The cost was prohibitive for just one person. The cost of the flight was generally shared by the team or several individuals.] So Deb keeps waiting. She's hoping to go on TAM (the military plane) Friday a.m., weather permitting. It's much too expensive to take the mission plane to Bahía Negra if there aren't others to help share the cost of the flight. Of course, in an emergency, you call the plane regardless.

We went to bed and barely got to sleep when our pilot called for Fred to pick him up (11:45 p.m.) at a Colonel's house. He had run out of gas with the motorbike and said there was a "takeover" in the government and some revolution out at the Cavalry; he needed to get off the street. It was hard to get back to sleep after hearing a revolution was taking place. We heard some shots and a jet taking off in the middle of the night. It was super low; we only heard it once. We learned later that President Stroessner was taken out of the country.

February 3rd: It's a Paraguayan holiday, but no parties will be allowed today. All Americans have been told to stay home and off the streets for the next few days. General Rodriguez took over the government. When he spoke on the radio he said all was peaceful and under control; and that President Stroessner was deprived of his liberty, but that he was in good health and being given his *rights*. [President Stroessner was actually General Rodriguez's father-in-law.]

For now all flights are canceled, and no one is allowed to go anywhere. According to the newspaper on the "takeover," there was more damage done and more lives lost of soldiers and police than initially reported.

February 4th: All seems "normal," but we've not been downtown where—according to the radio and TV—multitudes of young people are happily celebrating the happenings of the 3rd, as are the Catholics. Both groups are excited about the overthrow of President Stroessner. But do these people really understand what "democracy" means?

*****

The traffic downtown was terrible after the takeover. The big Catholic Church downtown was full to overflowing because of a funeral for all of the dead soldier boys—and there were thousands of them. They were stacked up like cordwood at the Military Hospital, with parents going there to identify their sons as they had no identification on them. How awful! There were bullet holes all over some of the buildings downtown.

*****

Deb and Heather finally got a flight home three weeks after their first try. It's a good thing they got off when they did, as the weather turned unstable again.

*****

We badly needed more personnel in Asunción. Everyone was too busy to fulfill all that was required of the town team. I had been praying that God would give wisdom concerning another family joining the Asunción team as buyer. It was difficult for the Asunción team to spend relaxed time with individuals who came in from the interior needing to talk.

Though those of us in town worked well together, everyone was carrying an extra heavy load; Fred had enough responsibility for three individuals. This made it very difficult when he was also expected to spend at least half his time visiting the stations. Sometimes the needs were such he had to spend more time than that traveling. The thinking had been to keep as many people as possible working among the indigenous tribal people. This meant keeping the town staff to as few people as possible, but the responsibilities of the town team had grown over the years with more government paperwork and other requirements, along with the outside opposition and missionaries seemingly needing more time spent with them for encouragement, counsel, and so on.

The consultant traveling was exhausting because there were so many places people expected us to be at the same time; some trips had to be rescheduled because of Fred's responsibilities in town. Rarely a day went by that we didn't have company—and sometimes multiple times in the day. I was feeling stretched rather thin, and for the first time I began seeing it affect Fred also.

We badly needed more co-workers. Even if we didn't have any less to do ourselves, we would not have to be overly concerned that the others didn't have enough help. That in itself would have eased my mind—just to know that others were satisfied and missionaries living in the interior weren't feeling neglected.

*****

There's not enough room to tell a lot of things the missionaries have to face on a daily basis. It's enough to say that life is unpredictable. I know that is true of life anywhere, but I think it takes a bit more of a flexible mindset to live the missionary life—if you're going to do so without a lot of frustration and tears. We must remain flexible and available—not knowing what we may be called upon to do next—yet diligent to pursue the work God has given us to do, regardless of the interruptions, the opposition and onslaughts of the enemy by whatever means he can conjure up. If he can't cause division within families, he'll try between co-workers or among the indigenous people with whom the missionaries are working. The most important thing the missionary must do is keep his or her time alone with the Lord the highest priority, and then to keep *short accounts* with all those with whom they live and work.

NTM missionaries have all been taught to faithfully practice biblical conflict resolution principles, so that makes a big difference in how problems are dealt with. That doesn't mean there's never conflict, but it's not allowed to go unresolved.

We had been on a station in the interior and were flying back to the Filadelfia flight base with hopes of returning home to Asunción, when we were called to stop at another station that was requesting our help and attention because of personnel problems. After talking over the situation with the members on the station, we ended up taking into our home one of the single girl missionaries who was in need of encouragement, rest, counsel, and love. We called our headquarters in the United States and talked to leadership there about keeping her in our home for a few months, rather than sending her back to the States defeated. It meant sometimes spending many hours a day with her on my part; but as we weaned her away from us and sent her to live at the guesthouse, where she began working in the print shop, we saw her again encouraged and blossom into a productive, happy individual. When she returned to the States on furlough at the end of the year, she got some professional help, which she said was a tremendous blessing and help to her. She later married and remained in the United States.

Sometimes when people in the home country hear about problems that can occur on the mission field—be it between missionaries, within families, or with those they may be working with—we have found some people to be shocked, thinking missionaries should be beyond such difficulties. Missionaries aren't super saints that never have problems. They are as human as the next person is. But because they have a desire to please the Lord and to be "sold out" for His using, they become a ready target for the enemy to attack. Satan works doubly hard to see ministers of the gospel defeated, because he doesn't want the gospel to be spread to those who've never had a chance to hear. He loves smear campaigns that ruin the testimonies of Christians—and specifically ministers of the gospel. We have seen it take place plenty of times right here in the United States.

*****

On April 19, 1989, Steve called to say that he and Monica were now the proud parents of a baby boy—Jason Kootenay Sammons; Jason's middle name was taken from Fred's dad.

*****

On April 24, Fred had an interview with British TV cameramen who were out to smear NTM and help the opposition. They were only taking pictures of the most negative kind—nothing of the progress and helps to the Indian. It was a blessing to remember that God is still in control. My prayer that day was that the Lord fill Fred's mouth with wisdom from above as He filled Balaam's mouth in the Old Testament.

With already having the pressures of insufficient personnel and being overburdened with the work load, it didn't help to have the outside opposition constantly harassing the mission, trying to get the missionaries kicked out of the country. The people who don't believe in God and don't want missionaries to work with the indigenous people, are desperate to do anything they can to smear the work. They seemingly feel no shame or guilt for creating lies in order to reach their objective.

*****

On April 29, 1989, Dave and Tammy arrived in Asunción with two other couples from Ramona, California, to frame up a house for a missionary joining the team at San Carlos. Because of bad weather they couldn't fly into the station until May 2, so the men put a sub-ceiling in our bedroom—which was very much appreciated. One couple, the Butlers, returned to Paraguay for a brief visit in March 1998, going back with us after our furlough time spent in Ramona.

Dave and Tammy Sammons
with
Bart and Sherry Butler
and
Al and Lyn Jaggi
(all from Ramona, California)

Fred, John, Jim, and Dora all went to San Carlos to help with the building. Dora went to do the cooking for the team. If only you could see the pictures from the video camera they took along. They worked in mud because of all the rains; the visitors from California had never worked with such crooked lumber. The family they went to help was grateful for what they were able to do in the short time they were there.

Dave and Tammy left to return home to California on May 18. The other two couples from the work team had left a week earlier. It was so much fun to have Dave and Tammy with us, along with the Woods and the Van Allens all at the same time—a very rare treat!

God's ways simply are not our ways.
His methods are not men's methods.
His estimate of things is diametrically
different from ours.
Not until we let go of what we own does it
become God's to do with as He chooses.

Thoughts from "Mighty Man of Valor"
by Phillip Keller

On June 1, 1989, Dora came to town bringing Jonathan with her. Jim and the other two boys stayed on the station. Dora was not supposed to lift Jonathan; she had another high-risk pregnancy. It was hard to see her leave to return to the station. I felt like crying all day after she and the baby left. I didn't see how she could possibly keep up with things in her present condition without more help. And I was not able to be that help. How I wished I could be. Fred went to the Ache village on business on June 9, returning to Asunción two days later, and he said Dora was doing okay while he was there.

A month later one of her co-workers came to town and said Dora wasn't doing well at all, didn't look well, but was busy trying to take care of the medical work. I went out with Paul Heckart, who was returning that night to the station to see if there was anything I could do to help, at least temporarily. Jim and Dora had no idea I was going out.

For some reason I don't remember now, they didn't have a washing machine that was working. The Ache girl who had been helping Dora in the house and with the laundry had taken off to the woods and hadn't returned. So I helped clean house, washed the laundry by hand each day, and did whatever I could to be of help for six days.

That station was a hard place to be for several reasons, one of them being because of the outside pressures of opposition to missionary work. It was no wonder Dora was worn out. The medical work on a mission station is a heavy responsibility at any time; it was especially hard for Dora because of her own physical condition. I was up at night multiple times with the kids. It was enough to make a well person sick. The baby was evidently teething; the others needed to go potty. Dora could have used a full-time nursemaid about then.

When Jim went out to pick up a package of medicine for Dora that had been sent from Asunción, there was a note for me from Fred. He had a visiting missionary's son with him for a couple days at our house, a young man from Bolivia.

Elsa (the Ache girl) returned from the woods and was back to help Dora again. I decided to go home. I couldn't change anything that was going to give any long-term help. It hurt to know how difficult it was for them all. Jim took me out by motorbike to where I could catch a bus back to Asunción. After being home I kept wondering about Dora and praying for her. No matter how you look at it, life isn't easy or simple for a young mother with several children, nor is it going to be for a few years to come; and I daresay it's harder yet in an Indian village where one has constant demands from the Indians to take care of them too. I never heard Dora complain.

At the end of July, John and Deb came to town with John very sick. Wow! Talk about the enemy at work to discourage missionaries in their ministries. Things I have mentioned here that happened with our adult kids are just examples of what might take place for any young couple in ministry on the mission field.

From Daily Bread: *Bumps are for climbing. God can turn obstacles into opportunities.*

Not too long after this, things got so "hot" with the opposition that the mission pulled out the missionaries from the Ache work at Cerro Morotĩ. A couple of the families moved to a small town nearby, where they could still have contact with the Ache until it was more clear what was to be done about that work. Jim and Dora relocated to the Pira station, where Dora again took care of the medical work.

September 1989

On September 2, after spending three weeks alone working on the Angaite language analysis at San Carlos, Fred joined me, and we then left San Carlos for our Filadelfia flight base. I was ready to go home, but we got a radio message from another station asking that we *please* go visit them. So there we were on the Santa Rosa station on September 4.

On the fifth, we learned by radio that Jessica Lynn Van Allen was born to Deb and John at 8:30 a.m. in Asunción. I was so disappointed to not be there to help John and Deb. The team at Santa Rosa had begged us to stop there before returning to Asunción. I had promised John I would be there when the baby was born, and I had promised Deb I would be there this time. I felt terrible about *not* being there. I couldn't be there for the first baby, but it seemed inexcusable to not be there when we were in the same country. People on the Santa Rosa station were disappointed when I cried wanting to be in Asunción with Deb rather than be at Santa Rosa right then [but wait till it's *their* turn]. Jessica was born ahead of the doctor's due date calculation.

Life sure seems hard sometimes. When we have choices to make and feel we've made the choice God would have us make at the time, I have to believe that the God who knows the future and how badly I wanted to be there, allowed things to go as they did, even though I may not understand the *why* of it all. It was not by choice that I missed special family times like this.

November 30, 1989, Jeffery Paul Wood was born by Caesarean section, weighing only 4 lbs. He was taken an extra month early, but the doctor said they had to take him when they did because the placenta was deteriorating. Jeffery had problems with his lungs for years even though Dora was given injections that were to help his lungs develop before he was born.

In early December, the missionaries from the interior came into town to attend the annual field conference, so John and Deb were back in town—John with a bad eye from a nail having punctured the white part of his eye. He ended up having surgery. It cost a lot of money, but at least his eye should be okay. Talk about a busy household, with six little kids and two sick adults! Dora was recuperating from her surgery; the baby wasn't sleeping well, so Dora was up much of the night. Those days before conference were busy with family, kids, visitors, and just trying to keep up with things in the house. The weather was super-hot and uncomfortable for those not feeling well, but conference time was a blessing. We celebrated Christmas as a family early before John and Deb returned to their station. I hit the "50" mark that year—right after Christmas. Unbelievable!

Year 1990

JANUARY 1990

Another year is dawning: Dear Father, let it be,
In working or in waiting, another year with Thee;
Another year of progress, another year of praise,
Another year of proving Thy presence all the days.

Another year of mercies, of faithfulness and grace,
Another year of gladness in the shining of Thy face;
Another year of leaning upon Thy loving breast,
Another year of trusting, of quiet, happy rest.

Another year of service, of witness for Thy love;
Another year of training for holier work above.
Another year is dawning: Dear Father, let it be,
On earth or else in heaven, another year for Thee.
(from Daily Bread)

    I was having my devotions one morning, thinking about all the interruptions that seem to come constantly. I had *just* written in my journal, "How I desire that God be the director of all my concerns, my schedule, etc." when Fred came home bringing someone else to visit. How often do we say one thing to the Lord, believing it to be our true heart's desire—and when God takes us at our word, we balk or feel disappointed, realizing we didn't really have in mind what HE had in mind for us that day. I always had to consider that what seemed like interruptions to me could well be *divine appointments* ordained by Him. And I often rejoiced, after the fact, at the blessing of those appointments chosen by Him.

    Apart from consultant travel and other usual responsibilities, there were times when indigenous people, coming into Asunción for medical help, needed to be picked up from the port and taken to the military hospital or the Indian department. Some of them we even kept in our home to see that they took their medications properly and got taken to where they needed to go for appointments and got back onto a boat to return home when they were finished. There were times when we were the only missionaries in town who spoke Guarani, and the Indians coming in didn't speak Spanish, which meant we were the ones chosen to take care of business for them and with them. There was no time to get bored that is for sure.

    On March 4, we heard that Deb had been bitten by a poisonous snake up in Bahía Negra, but that it barely broke the skin. When I was talking to Deb later, she said they decided to use a stun gun on her anyhow; she said they would have to catch her next time. The stun gun has been used effectively with poisonous bites and stings to neutralize the poison somehow.

While on a boat on the way to San Carlos, I read *Keep Climbing*, by Gail MacDonald, and I was impressed with some of the thoughts she shared. She mentions several excellent analogies about our need for "spiritual sharpening." Imagine cutting with a dull machete. The *time out* for sharpening is not an interruption in the work, but part of the work—and most needful for effective work thereafter. This book also brings out the need for our eyes to be riveted on the Master for His direction in our service to Him.

The need is for such a relationship with Him that we are aware *He* is in control of all situations in our lives—not holding illusions as to what can or cannot happen to us. Not putting God in a box, realizing what humanity really is, therefore judging no one else. No room for hate. Looking for the face of Christ in the face of other believers, rather than judging the negative things we see. Not desiring to vindicate ourselves when others have hurt us, be it consciously or unconsciously. Living according to God's standard—not influenced by the expectations of man. Our need to learn how to be a "comforter/friend" to another who may be suffering. Listening, caring, praying for, not *preaching at* (though faithful as a friend)—not liking the person any less for their failure.

The analogy is given of Christ with His disciples at the Lord's last supper. Would we so willingly have sat there fellowshipping with those we knew would betray us? Or, would we get up and leave in disgust? The Lord knew what would happen; yet He was patient and loving. He understood humanity. It was for this He must die.

But we who are so unrighteous ourselves quickly judge others. May we learn to love with a love that is Christ-like—not dependent upon another's performance or their liking or disliking us. Our responses must be Christ-like regardless, if we expect God's blessing on our lives.

On this particular boat trip, a bad wind and rainstorm blew up while we were in the dining area having a cup of coffee. Fred went to shut the window in our room; water was pouring in. Some things got wet, including my bed and leather tote bag. We sat in the dining room until the bad winds passed. Several small children on the boat were frightened. The boat docked for a short while, then continued on. We spent a few days at San Carlos and then traveled by mission plane to a few other stations before returning home to Asunción.

On the May 11, John and Heather came in to go to the dentist. John tried numerous times to get back home by TAM plane and for one reason or another, the plane didn't go. Then the plane did go, got all the way to Bahía Negra, but it didn't land. Deb heard the plane. The news was that the airstrip was wet, but Deb said it was dry. John said the plane was heavily loaded, and the pilot was possibly too inexperienced to land in that situation. Deb was so discouraged. She said their motor was out, she had to do laundry by hand, carrying water by bucket, the weather had turned super cold, and John wasn't there to help. He and Heather weren't able to get home until May 22. No lack of opportunities to learn patience and endurance!

In August of 1990, Fred, along with a fellow co-worker, left for the United States for meetings at our NTM headquarters. Some problems had surfaced amongst some co-workers on one of the stations; as a result, some misunderstandings had developed, and two of our field leaders went to headquarters to talk with the mission executive committee members.

Fred was so positive concerning what the outcome would be in talking to the mission leaders. We both felt strongly that God was in charge, and whatever He did was okay. But I found myself feeling a bit apprehensive after Fred left. I had a strange feeling deep inside that something hard was going to take place. I didn't want to fight the Lord's will for us in any way, but I wasn't wanting to leave Paraguay; mention had been made of such a possibility by a couple individuals. There had been some unfortunate misunderstandings, but Fred always says, "God keeps the books." The enemy's attacks were many during those days; it seemed there was to be no let-up. We felt that, in time, things would be made right; and if not, God knew, and He was in control regardless.

When Fred returned from the meetings in the States, he just said to me, "This is a closed chapter in my life; I don't want to discuss it anymore." He was relieved, though hurt. He would be free to do more traveling and have more time to study and teach, which he liked to do. He had asked for more help a long time back, but it wasn't forthcoming until this took place; not exactly as planned, but as it turned out we did get more help; Fred was replaced with three individuals—not all immediately, but over a short period of time. We had been understaffed for far too long. Someone else came from another field to function as field director.

As long as we are humans on this earth, we will face difficulties with relationship problems from time to time; not all of them will turn out as we would like them to. We always have a choice, however, as to what our response will be in the midst of the problems. There are always positive things to learn from any negative situation; and where the attitude remains good, there can be growth and an appreciation of the fact that God never changes, and His love toward us never changes. Why would we *give up* and quit because of personal difficulties, refusing to continue to serve where He has placed us when He has been forever faithful to us? He never promised this life would be easy and without hurts. He is not surprised by men's failures, it's we who are. Our prayer was that God make us better servants of His as a result of the difficult situation we were experiencing.

The following month I read a book by Tim Hansel, *You Gotta Keep Dancin*, in reference to living with pain and disappointments. I appreciated the reminder that contentment and joy do not hinge on circumstances.

On August 18, Steve, Monica and children arrived for a visit from California. It was wonderful to have them with us. Though Fred was unable to go along, they and I went to Pira to visit Jim, Dora, and the boys. John and Deb came to town to see them, as Deb was scheduled to have gallbladder surgery on September 5—the day Steve and Monica left to return home.

𝒫salms 84:11 "No good thing will He withhold from them that walk uprightly."

Journal entry:

It seems like so much of what I'm reading these days has to do with comfort from the Lord, and joy and peace in the midst of adversity. Decisions are being made that I do not understand, but my prayer is, "Lord, help us to remain faithful—with a Christ-like spirit."

On September 21, Steve called to talk to his dad. He wanted to let his dad know he appreciates his attitude to "stick in" and not give up. He said that he himself had been looking for the perfect situation and realizes such doesn't exist, and that his dad's example has been helpful to him. Steve is obviously growing and stretching too; it's a blessing to see his positive response.

In reading in Philippians one day in October about our lives being *sincere,* I was reminded of how we've often used the lesson from Spanish of the word *sin cera*—without wax, authentic—not covering the cracks, pretending to be something we're not—which reminds me of what has been said of a potter molding clay. Some things crack as they go through the fire; the potter may fill the cracks with wax, polish over it, and the average person would never recognize it had ever been cracked. Held up to the light, the crack would show through—sun tested. In respect to us as individuals, speaking of spiritual truths, we would say "SON tested."

On December 26, Steve called to say they had a new baby girl, Ashley Nicole Sammons, our 9th grandchild.

On December 27, I spent seven hours at the hospital with a new missionary couple; the wife had C-section surgery and needed someone there who could speak the language for her if necessary. I did some proofing on the Angaite language analysis part of the time.

Fred is seen here with three of Steve and Monica's kids: Janelle, Jason, and Ashley. Fred came to the United States on committee business, so he was able to see the grandkids at the same time.

"Take away the dross from the silver, and there shall come forth a vessel for the finer."
𝒫roverbs 25:4

16
Year 1991

January 1st, my journal said the following:

> I'm still reading *Grace Awakening*, by C. Swindoll. Excellent book! How I desire to be a "yes" person, not a grace killer. What I read today had to do with making comparisons with others. We need to let others *be* and accept ourselves as God made *us* to be. How I pray our town team will bind together in love and unity and be able to work comfortably together. We are still in a transition period with new leaders, but things seem to be working smoothly.

It was hard living in Asunción while trying to do language work for people living in the interior at the same time. People who came to visit would say, "You're always working." They didn't seem to realize that although I was glad to take a break with them when they came, they would probably find me at work upon arrival. Because I did have a job to do, I couldn't just go to the guesthouse to sit for hours on end, just visiting. Although they were *on break*, I was not. It was impossible to be everything to everyone and to meet everyone's expectations. And that was hard for me, as someone who wants to please and "fix" everything.

March 1991

March 4, we were on a trip to the interior and had been visiting several different stations. This particular day we were in Santa Rosa in the Manjúi village, and it was raining. We were invited to have lunch with one of the missionary families. Their young daughter, Janie, had come over to the place we were staying as guests, so Fred picked her up and put her on his shoulders to take her home. He said, "It isn't every day I get to pick up a pretty little girl." He barely got that out of his mouth when he took a step, slipped, and fell in the mud. I went to get Janie (who was angry about being dropped in the mud, but wasn't hurt) and I fell. It didn't hurt me much, just twisted my back and neck a bit. But Fred was really stiff. It knocked the wind out of him; it was scary. His face turned blue; we weren't sure he was going to be okay, initially. He was very stiff and sore on the side he fell on. We figured it was just bruised ribs. He didn't go to the doctor, but it seemed likely some ribs were cracked; it was weeks before he could fully dress himself. An x-ray taken years later revealed a badly shattered hip. And whether or not the Paget's disease he has since been diagnosed with is a result of that accident or not, we will never know. We did learn later that Fred's dad actually had Paget's disease (a bone disease that in some cases causes a lot of disfigurement), but it obviously had little effect on Dad physically, as we never even knew he had it until after he had died of other causes.

God's grace keeps pace with whatever we face.

June 1991

We were visiting the missionaries in San Carlos again; I was again working on the Angaite language analysis. The bugs were absolutely terrible. I had acquired chigger bites that itch like crazy and on top of that the polvorine (no seeums) were thick and biting till I felt like I was on fire.

While at San Carlos, I was reading *Trusting God Even when Life Hurts*, by Jerry Bridges; he brings out that God owes us no explanation for adversity. We may or may not see and understand His purposes in time. It is enough to know He is in control. Job never did know the *why* of what happened to him, but he did indicate a deeper relationship with God because of his trials.

As to understanding the *whys* of things, it is certainly always difficult to understand what's happening among so many professing Indian believers, who are listening to those in opposition of the gospel and the missionaries. The opposition will go to any length to lie and misinterpret the purpose of the missionary being here. That's hard to take when we could live much more comfortably in our own country if our purpose were just *living*.

It's often discouraging to give of oneself and see so few results—or see negative results and not know what to do about it. We can only throw ourselves on the Lord and trust Him to work as He sees fit, but we can't be fatalistic about it. We must pray for His working in *our* lives. May He also work in the lives of these people.

On June 19, a radio message from the Asunción office said a fax from Dave and Tammy said she's pregnant—a real answer to prayer. I'll bet they were so excited! They were told by the doctors they would never have children of their own. This was after almost ten years of marriage.

On June 27, Fred took his turn going with one of the Angaite men to meet a boat out in the middle of the river that was to bring the station supplies. They left at 8:00 p.m. to meet the Cacique boat, but I was surprised at 4:30 a.m. to realize Fred hadn't yet returned. There was some rain and a cold south wind; it was not good weather to go out in, but one goes when the boat is passing by, regardless of the weather if you know the supplies have been put on that boat by the Asunción buyer. As it turned out, Fred and Mario returned around 5:00 a.m. with no supplies. No boat had come by. We were all disappointed—no mail!

It can be super cold at this time of year; we kept a fire in the barrel stove in the San Carlos guesthouse to at least take off the chill. Though it doesn't heat up the back room, and drafts are everywhere, it sure beats having no heat!

Fred did an excellent job teaching in the Indian church about the believer's standing and responsibility to keep clean God's temple—not quenching the Holy Spirit.

God's requirements are met by God's enablement.
God doesn't comfort us to make us comfortable, but to make us comforters.

Notes from my Journal
July 1991

Fred went to Concepción to take care of business that had to do with the San Carlos land title and came back again. A colony meeting was called, and Fred talked to everyone about the plans for NTM to transfer the land title to the Angaite. The opposition was telling them it was never going to happen. One day I feel like God is so at work; and I'm sure He is. But the outward appearance of how things are going presently doesn't seem terribly positive. Inocencio went off and got drunk Sunday afternoon; it's one person after another like that.

It's so buggy and the lighting so poor, I can't study. I end up going to bed earlier than normal because I can't see to do anything else.

On July 15, I went to the airstrip to see Fred off—a bit of a strange feeling— him leaving and me staying on here at San Carlos to work. I don't think I'll ever get used to it. It's one thing his having to travel, leaving me home; but quite another when I'm somewhere alone that is *not* home. I was working on the morphology of the Angaite language. Things were slowly coming together concerning the contractions—mostly a process of assimilation and fusing.

On July 27, my journal says: It's hard to believe this is my last day here. I have mixed feelings about leaving. I want to be with Fred, but I hate to leave the work here. It is so needy! I worked hard a.m. to clean the guesthouse; I gave away anything extra I had—food, clothes, whatever. Everything is ready to close up, but I kept the computer out to do some more work and give JS last-minute copies. I feel my time this last two weeks was worth the staying. The 'biggies' seem to be *in hand* and falling into place. How good the Lord is. He has taught me so much through this analytical work, though it has not been easy, to say the least.

I got on the Cacique about midnight; they were ready for me as Fred had paid for the room in Asunción. They immediately took me to Room 3, gave me a key, and put in my things, and I lay down and slept. Not bad; tiny room, narrow, thin mattress—but great to have a place to rest. Sure was glad Fred took care of it at the other end.

I was on that boat until the morning of the 29th—not eating or drinking anything. I had tried once to go get a cup of coffee the afternoon of the 28th, but the kitchen was closed and no hot water was available. Being the only foreigner on the boat—and being a woman alone—I attracted too much attention, so I didn't brave going again. I stayed in the room until about 5:00 a.m. Monday, when we arrived in Asunción. Fred was there at the boat docks waiting for me. I was sure glad to see him!

August 1991

August 5: I was reading a borrowed book *Through the Wilderness of Loneliness*, by Tim Hansel. It's amazing how sometimes one can feel lonely, even amid friends or family; God meets special needs and areas in our lives at times like this, too—causing us to be more sensitive to Him and to His leading—also causing us to be more caring and sensitive to the needs of those around us.

August 10: I read an interesting little story in *Daily Bread* today about two goats meeting on a high, dangerous ridge where they couldn't back up. Finally one knelt down and made himself as flat as possible, allowing the other goat to walk over him. You know, we need to be humble enough to do the same in real-life situations here.

August 25: I had a discussion with someone else in leadership about the Spanish language learning program for married women with children. It was said that the goal should be to speak so well one can be mistaken for a native speaker—which I feel is an unrealistic goal for the majority of people. As much as I wish it were true, it is rare. I believe we should work toward effective, understandable communication to the extent that our foreignness is not an issue.

September 1991

September 8: The song *It Is Well with My Soul* was singing through my mind this a.m. I'm thankful my soul indeed is at peace with the Lord. I am sure feeling some pressure, however, on the language analysis. I keep having so many interruptions.

September 19: Fred left for Filadelfia at 2 p.m. I sat in the NTM office for two hours, listening for the phone. We staff women take turns in the afternoons staying by the phone in the main office.

I listened to a tape of Jim and Dora's presentation today. I finished the Angaite Gospel Story booklet today and took it to the print shop.

September 23: I finished reading a book my niece loaned me on *How to Get Along With Difficult People*. Enlightening to say the least! I have some work to do on myself!

September 26: Tomorrow is our 33rd anniversary. I hope Fred can call from Filadelfia. It has been nice talking to him via radio every day, but it's not very private on his end.

September 29: I had a nice visit with Fred at 2 p.m., along with a couple other missionaries on the radio frequency.

*****

In November, Fred was gone to our headquarters in Sanford, Florida, for eleven days on business, along with some others from the field. It was nice to get pictures of the kids from Dora when Fred returned. They were on furlough at the time, as were John and Deb. How I missed the kids!

*****

In December we received a letter from John about having broken his leg and how he woke from surgery quoting Psalm 23.

17
Year 1992

Jesse David Sammons was born on January 29, 1992, to Dave and Tammy. Jesse is our tenth grandchild and a direct answer to prayer. The doctor had said Dave and Tammy would never have children of their own. After ten years of marriage and much prayer, Jesse was born.

*****

While on a visit to San Carlos in February, I wrote,

These Angaite people look so ragged and dirty here, depressed, discouraged, etc. I see these little people around here that could be as loving as my own grandchildren, if only they had the same opportunities. And the thought came to me—my own grandchildren will probably never cry out of honest hunger. I am sure some of these kids do experience hunger. Many of them are malnourished. This is a sad place. Life is so hard for these Angaite people. I haven't had much time to visit with the Angaites themselves because we've been in meetings with the missionaries. Not sure if there will be time to do much visiting, but I will want to do some.

I read the book of Jonah today. It's interesting how Jonah, as God's messenger, desired evil to fall upon the people of Nineveh rather than being happy about their repentance. Yet God was merciful. Do we love people unconditionally as God does? Can we see people through Christ's eyes as HE sees them?—men, women and children for whom He died.

It is super-hot tonight. I'm *dripping*! It's still and humid, with no breeze at all.

Entries of that type into my journal were rather common. One never gets used to seeing extreme poverty and malnutrition. And as for the weather, the bugs, and other irritations, one doesn't get used to that either. It's something one learns to live with, and hopefully without complaining, but you don't learn to *like* it. Is it worth putting up with all of that to see people come to know the Lord and learn to walk with Him? YES! POSITIVELY, YES!

I Corinthians 3:13 "Every man's work shall be made manifest: ...it shall be revealed by fire; and the fire shall try every man's work of what sort it is."

I Corinthians 4:2 "...it is required in stewards, that a man be found faithful."

March 1992

We arranged to buy John and Deb's car for $2,000 for them to pay their tickets back to Paraguay—selling our car to other missionaries here.

*****

Some of the young wives are having a hard time because of the stress of caring for young children, along with household chores being more difficult here. They feel they could do those things in the United States with less frustration—and there would not be language study to worry about either. They are forgetting their husband's role and the need to be supportive of him.

I have always said it isn't the heat and the bugs that send missionaries home from the field, but I do have to say that those things tend to magnify the difficult situations. The truth is that most of the young wives who struggle with such thoughts would never want to quit and return to their homeland defeated. They just need someone to talk to, someone to encourage them, and people back home to faithfully pray for them to be encouraged in the Lord. He has promised to be faithful to meet *every* need; and He will, as we lean upon Him to do so.

*****

April 17, 1992 — February 14, 1993

We arrived back to the United States for a ten-month *home assignment*. As we returned to the United States, it was time for both our kids and their families to return to Paraguay. We all met at Dave and Tammy's in Ramona, California. Poor Dave and Tammy! They had a big house at that time, and we were all enjoying being together again. Steve and Monica lived in Santee, not that far away—so *all* of us had some good times together.

John and Deb were still at Dave and Tammy's until April 28. Jim and Dora were the first to leave for Paraguay, leaving a few days after our arrival. They went back a month early for Dora to have a needed major surgery. Doctors here had told her she needed the surgery; the cost would be $15,000. The same surgery at that time cost her $1,000 in Paraguay at the Baptist Hospital.

The first time I went to a supermarket here, I was surprised at how much variety there was of everything and how clean everything looked. I thought the supermarkets we had by then in Asunción were nice. But I was reminded of a conversation I had with a new missionary on the field. When I indicated our supermarkets in Asunción were comparable to those in the United States, the person asked how long it had been since I had been in the States, and then let me know that I had forgotten what a supermarket in the United States was like.

I see in my journals while on furlough that more than once I stated I wished we could have a place of our own so we'd not be a burden to others. Missionaries always have so much *stuff* around that it has to be a nuisance. It was hard enough for us; I can only imagine that it was much worse for the people with whom we were staying.

*****

It was during this furlough that I enrolled with Lael College and Graduate School out of St. Louis, Missouri—thanks to our son Steve's encouragement.

July 1992

July 1, 1992, the field chairman in Paraguay called and said they wanted the Jantz family to move to town on a permanent basis, which would certainly lighten the town load for the staff there; and we were free to go to San Carlos to live. That changed how we needed to plan concerning what to take or not take back with us as we return to Paraguay. The Jantz family would live in the Asunción house we had been living in.

Some people thought we wouldn't like to return to the interior to live on a more permanent basis because of our ages, particularly in the hot, buggy Chaco, but we were both happy about the opportunity to make that move—not because of the heat and bugs, of course.

We had asked earlier if we could move to San Carlos when one of the families retired from that station, but our Asunción co-workers would hear nothing of it. They felt they needed Fred in Asunción because he *knew the ropes* of everything there. And I felt that was a good reason for Fred to move, because someone younger needed to be trained into those responsibilities that only Fred was proficient at before it was too late. So, the move was an answer to prayer for us.

During this furlough time, we did a lot of traveling to visit friends, family, and supporters—having meetings in various churches—and were involved in daily Vacation Bible School for a week in our home church. Fred spoke at the NTM Bible Institutes as well as the Language Institute, challenging the students to reach the unreached. We spent some time at the NTM Medical Center for dental work. We traveled 22,000 miles over a period of four months.

We spent some time taking care of grandkids while their parents were busy or traveling; I did as much college study as possible when time was available. I even studied on a small laptop in the car as we traveled from one place to another.

On December 18, I took two CLEP exams at the National University in San Diego, Algebra and English (and passed). Those subjects were required by Lael College; they accepted the results of the CLEP exams.

From January 14–30, we took a computer course at our mission headquarters in Sanford, Florida. We kept busy thereafter with attending meetings, visiting with Mom Sammons in the nursing home, shopping with retired missionaries at the retirement center—helping them get their place set up, and collecting packages people wanted to send with us to their family or friends in Paraguay.

Home Assignment completed.

It was good to get back to Paraguay. I was prepared for things to look tacky after being in the United States where things are so nice, but no place looked better than home to me when we got back. I could imagine how good it felt for Dave and Tammy to have their home to themselves once again.

Fred spoke at the first Sunday evening meeting after we arrived back to Asuncion. All the missionaries who were in town gathered together for evening fellowship; and I played the piano for singing. The mission had bought a piano for the meeting room while we were gone. Nice!

HE MAKETH NO MISTAKE

My Father's way may twist and turn, my heart may throb and ache,
But in my soul I'm glad I know, He maketh no mistake.

My cherished plans may go astray, my hopes may fade away,
But still I'll trust my Lord to lead for He doth know the way.

Tho' night be dark and it may seem that day will never break;
I'll pin my faith, my all in Him, He maketh no mistake.

There's so much now I cannot see, my eyesight's far too dim;
But come what may, I'll simply trust and leave it all to Him.

For by and by the mist will lift and plain it all He'll make.
Through all the way, tho' dark to me, He made not one mistake.
—A.M. Overton

In Transition

Though we had permission to move to San Carlos, we didn't actually get to move there with all our things until the end of May.

While we were gone on furlough the termites decided to take over a cupboard in Fred's office and destroyed many of his books. We were busy trying to clean up that mess and get resituated after having been gone for several months.

We learned of the opportunity to attend a Cross-Cultural Communication seminar (for credit or audit), which would cost close to $145 to do for credit. Even auditing was expensive, $89. We planned to make one trip to the interior, then be back in time for the course, which was being taught by qualified professors from another mission—and from another country. I don't remember if we audited only or took the class for credit. I do know I did all the homework—even if it was only for auditing.

We did make a trip to the interior to visit one of the stations where I did some language checks. I spent time with one of the newer missionaries, who expressed his frustration at the interruptions in the village with having to care for Indian needs. I don't know the answer, because there will never be an ideal situation for doing God's work. We must be doing it in whatever situation He places us.

We returned to our flight base, where we went to an experimental farm and bought a few plants and fruit trees to take to plant at San Carlos. We went next to San Carlos to check out the house in which we would be living so we would know what we needed to take with us when we moved there.

No one had been living in the house for quite a while; I don't remember now just how long it had been since the previous owners had left in retirement. But the place needed a thorough cleaning and some good old TLC. Rats were running around the house—which was now ours. Fred killed two of them, but I saw two more that were too fast to get.

It was super-hot inside! We moved the bed from the bedroom to the living room and set it under the 12-volt ceiling fan (run by a battery hooked up to a solar panel). How thankful I was for all that the Woods (in-laws of Dora's) did in this house, especially the 12-volt lights and shower. I loved the jungle with all the trees and plants; the Woods had so many beautiful plants. Amazingly, many of the flowers were still there; no one had bothered them.

The old furniture in the house was so heavy I couldn't move most of it. I hurt my back trying. Most of it was made from rough lumber cut there at San Carlos. It wasn't the greatest looking furniture, but it worked well. I did a lot of cleaning on that first trip in and planned to paint once we got moved in.

I woke up the next morning about 3:00 a.m. and couldn't get back to sleep. At 4:00 a.m. I finally decided to just get up to read and pray. Different songs were running through my head as I lay in bed awake, like *I Must Tell Jesus, In the Garden, Constantly Abiding, No one Ever Cared for me like Jesus*, and the first few verses of Psalm 34 in Spanish. I could not remember all of verse 5. I finally decided to get up and review it. I made a cup of coffee and sat at Dene's old desk with her battery light. Another blessing! They left us so much here.

Fred planted several plants and trees and worked in the yard on this first trip. He hired the neighbor guy to clean out the brush to the river. Though it was not part of our yard, it affected our breeze (or lack of it, actually).

A branch of the river runs alongside the San Carlos property. I loved to go down there in the early morning, before people were milling around, and stand by the river and watch the sunrise.

I woke up the next day again at 2:30 a.m. It felt like evil around. Dogs were barking and would not shut up. I mentioned it to Fred; he prayed, and we went back to sleep. I didn't sleep soundly, but at least I did get some sleep. I got up at 5:00 a.m. There was a beautiful breeze off the river; it was quiet outside except for someone's rooster. I soon heard locusts out in the trees and some larger birds waking up. I would have liked to go see the river at that hour but wasn't dressed yet; it was just about sunrise...light out, and the birds were crying down at the river.

I did more housecleaning, cleaned the outside porch and swept down the outside walls. *It will soon look like home. I like it here. May we make friends!* I gave terere to a few people in the yard, as they sat down to drink and visit, waiting for the clinic to open.

We were only in San Carlos for three or four days at that time, but we got quite a lot of work done; we had a lot better idea of what we would need when we returned.

Both of us were exhausted after this trip. It was hot, humid, and just plain uncomfortable. I wrote up language reports from checks I had given—with copies to the field committee, the individuals checked, and to the South American representative.

We went to the Cross-cultural Communications class and enjoyed it. There were nineteen students. They were hoping for a twentieth student to round out small groups. I was in the small group that had only three people; the other two were men (one was South African; the other was American, with the Free Methodist mission).

When we got home from class we had a sandwich and got to work. I completed the required reading assignment first and then did some writing in a journal that had to be handed in to the professors. The one thing I didn't like about this course was having to grade ourselves. I had never done *that* before. Nor do I remember how I graded myself. I did keep a journal specifically for the Cross-Cultural Communication class. It was sixty typewritten pages (spaced at 1.5). I wish I had kept it; I haven't been able to find it again.

We had twelve days together as a class, finishing the last day by eating together at the home of one of the students who lived in Asunción. About a month later there was a reunion for those who had attended the Cross-Cultural class. One of the guys, who was in that class and heard we were moving to San Carlos, wanted to go to San Carlos to help us with the addition we planned to add onto the house. Amazing! We never even knew him before we took the culture class. We wanted to add an office and bedroom, hoping the new bedroom would receive more cross ventilation than the existing one, as that place was so hot.

We went to Pedro Juan Caballero and the Pira station in April. In between trips I was scrubbing 200-liter oil drums and packing in them. I also offered to spend several hours a day, and even a night, up at the hospital with a co-worker's daughter to spare the parents—for several days. I also did some canning to take to San Carlos. Fred was gone on a committee trip.

I gave many of my town dress clothes to one of the town co-workers who was my size and my dress heels to another co-worker in town. After we had moved to San Carlos, Jim and Dora were asked to go work in Asunción; one of her best friends said to her, "One person got your mom's clothes, another her shoes and someone else her house"—indicating Dora ended up with none of it. Dora just laughed. She was the same size as me too. I did send her a few things later. Dora didn't seem to mind what the others got; she loved her town co-workers.

Getting everything packed and ready to truck to the port to go by boat was a hassle for days. Jim and Dora were in town at the time, and Jim helped with getting our things wrapped and put on a truck, as well as helping load rock and sand that also had to be shipped for the foundation and the cement floor. Jim ended up breaking a finger with the rock handling.

Another young couple was moving to San Carlos at the same time we were; the guys went by boat with all our belongings. Barb and her kids and I went a bit later by bus to Filadelfia (the flight base) to fly into San Carlos by mission plane.

On May 28, all of my things were ready to leave the house for the last time. I walked through the house, cried, and then prayed, thanking the Lord for the place we'd had for the last six and a half years. It was the longest we had lived in any one place since we married. It was my prayer that the Jantzes would enjoy it as much as we had. I said goodbye to friends and to Jim, Dora, and kids. The little guys didn't want me to leave. Jantzes took us to the bus. It was a tearful goodbye.

The bus trip was uneventful to Filadelfia. Barb and her kids were fine. I held the baby off and on to give her a break. We stayed the night in the mission guesthouse.

We got to San Carlos by mission plane the next day about 4:30 p.m. It was a beautiful day. I put away some things and then went to supper with the team. They gave some leftovers to me for Sunday, as we would be busy working, getting things off the boat.

The next morning we woke up at 3:50 a.m. with a loud crash of thunder and some rain. We prayed it would stop until the boat was unloaded, as it was hard enough to get stuff up that hill and steep bank even without rain. I worked all day putting things away.

Our new co-workers organized things, and it all went much smoother than it would have otherwise; all the unloading was finished in one day. I was so glad it was over; it was kind of fun getting set up again. It was easy to make that place homey, as it is easier to make a rustic place look homey than a fancy place. I so wished Dora could see what I was doing; she would be glad for us (in her in-laws' house), as would Jim and Dene (the previous owners).

RG, whom we had met at the Cross-Cultural Communication course, was there to help us; he was one fantastic worker. We would never have finished things so quickly had he not been there. He stayed to work for almost two weeks. We were so grateful for his help. We offered to call the plane to take him out when he had to leave, but he insisted on going by boat—which was unfortunate in that he ended up very ill with hepatitis for months afterward from something he ate on the boat. Who could have known?

This is an early morning scene across from our house in San Carlos.

18
LIVING IN COLONIA SAN CARLOS

One month after we arrived in San Carlos to live, a Summit Team (Short-Term Missions group) arrived to help the new young family who had moved to the station at the same time we did. The Filadelfia administrator came also, staying at our place, to help with the oversight of the Summit Team work projects. An experienced couple from NTM headed the team up; most of the rest of the team were teenagers.

Whitney Michelle Sammons was born on July 2, 1993, to Steve and Monica; she is our eleventh grandchild—Steve and Monica's fourth child.

The addition to our place was quickly finished, thanks to the help of a friend from Asunción and our gracious co-workers. Painting and other odd jobs could be completed in the evenings and whenever there was time available. We were thrown into work responsibilities on the station immediately and were back to consultant travel within just a few weeks.

I continued with routine language checks throughout the field; Fred continued coordinating as well as being involved with the field committee—meaning he often traveled when I did not. I continued working on the Angaite language analysis and worked with the translator once he was into Bible-related lesson materials and Bible translation. I had previously translated Old Testament Bible story booklets from Guarani into Angaite (when making trips to San Carlos to work on the language) with the help of an Angaite language speaker.

Fred enjoyed traveling. It was good for him to get out and see what was happening on the other stations; he was grateful for a chance to get away from all the mosquitoes and other biting bugs we had in San Carlos. That station was known to be the worst on the field for all the bugs; missionaries from other stations just laughed when we invited them to take their "break" at San Carlos. I didn't like the bugs, either; but more frustrating to me were the bats, along with the termites and rats that ruined so many things.

Finding good language helpers was difficult; finances were tight, so it was initially impossible to hire anyone to help on a consistent basis. The language situation at San Carlos was complicated. All the people there spoke Guarani fluently. They had worked on ranches and had lived around the Paraguayans for many years, so they didn't lack vocabulary for speaking in Guarani. However, it was felt that the older people, who still knew and used their own language among themselves, didn't have as clear an understanding of the scripture in Guarani as they would have in Angaite; so it had been decided some years back that it was necessary to have a Bible translation in Angaite for those who were still freely using their own language. The problem was, there had never been a completed grammatical analysis of the language so as to know how to write it. It was part of my responsibility to see that happen. I did complete a Pedagogical Grammar in Angaite for the translators' use.

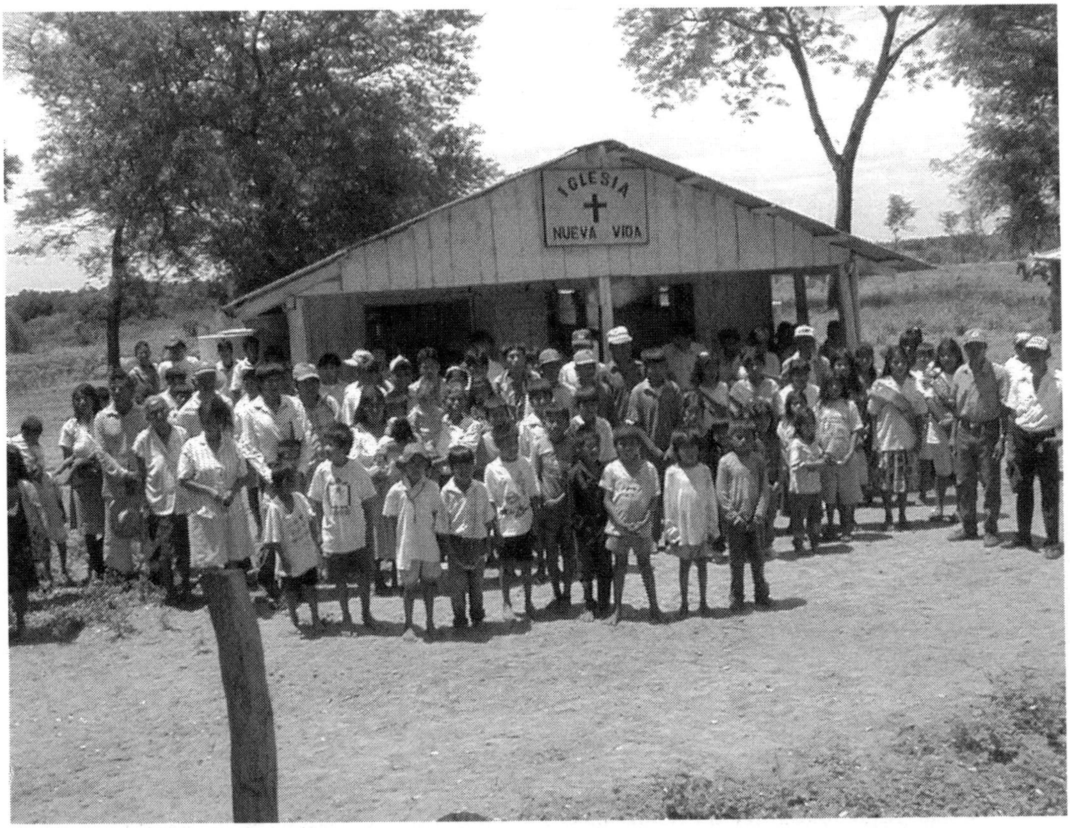
IGLESIA
NUEVA VIDA

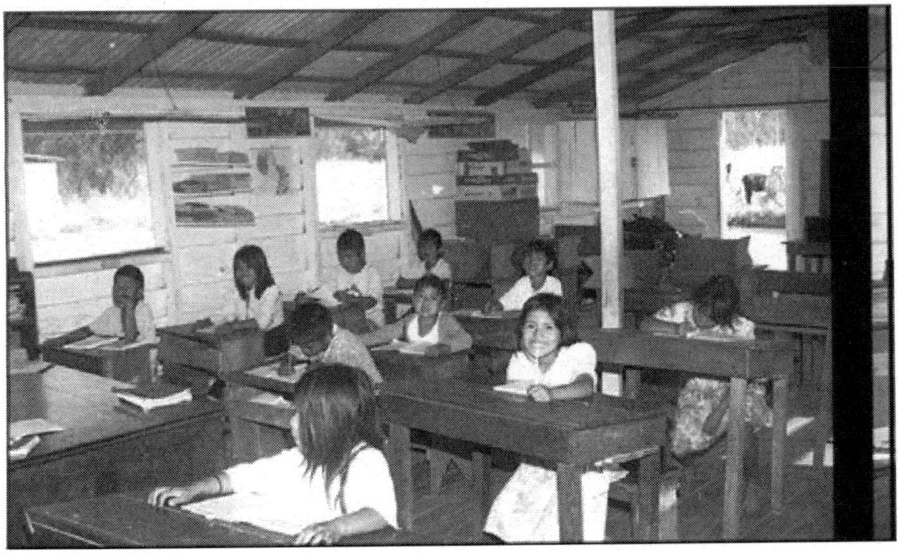

There were at least three dialects of Angaite present in the village; each one said theirs was the correct one and that the others were not the true Angaite language. In our presence they only spoke Guarani—no matter which group they were from, so it was extremely difficult to even learn the language. Much of the difference between dialects just involved contracted forms.

When I would get language from one dialect and use it on a person who happened to be of another dialect, they would correct me, saying that was not the true Angaite. Prior to moving to the station I had worked on some literacy materials in Angaite for the other missionaries to use in teaching some older people to read their language, and they had the same difficulty in trying to teach a literacy class where people from more than one dialect were present. Even if it was only an occasional word that was used differently from one group to the other, someone had to make an issue of it. It was somewhat frustrating to the person trying to teach.

When translating the Old Testament Bible stories into Angaite from Guarani, I had called together a representative of each of the dialects to do a read-through with them to be sure all understood the material before printing. We found only one or two words that were even in question, which we were able to replace with words acceptable to all; so we knew the problem was a prestige thing, nothing more. We chose to go with the dialect that was in the majority.

A few years later, the decision was made by our field leadership for the main translator to move to a location where the people were freely using their own language in everyday living. The young people at San Carlos did not speak Angaite, nor were they interested in doing so. They were more interested in mixing with their national neighbors and perfecting the use of that language.

Involvement of the missionaries at San Carlos included Bible teaching, discipling believers, overseeing a school from first through sixth grades with indigenous teachers, overseeing a store for the community with indigenous help, and running a medical clinic. The missionaries helped the people with personal needs in other ways as well.

On September 30, 1993, Fred and I left San Carlos by boat to go downriver to the town of Concepción, where we were to catch a military plane up to Bahía Negra. This was where John and Deb Van Allen were living and working among the Chamacoco Indians. I was going there to check the Bible translation of the Wycliffe missionary who was part of the team, working in association with the New Tribes missionaries there. The team always had a list of jobs they wanted Fred to help with when he went along.

The boat we had to catch out on the river came by late, so we were late arriving to Concepción the next day. We got there at the same time the TAM plane was at the airport preparing to leave for Bahía Negra; we had the agency call to find out if the plane would wait for us to get to the airport, but no way would they wait. So, it was Hotel Francés till Monday. We were both so tired that it was a relief to get some rest after that boat trip.

One is certainly aware of being a *gringo* in a place like this. You stick out like a sore thumb—as is true on the Aquidaban boat also; I never got used to being stared at.

Fred called Asunción from the hotel so they could tell John and Deb why we weren't on the plane. Then in the afternoon, Norm called from Asunción to say John and Deb had half their roof ripped off, and rain poured in, soaking everything from tornado winds. A tornado had done terrible damage the day before in the town of Benjamín Aceval, leaving 150 families homeless, damaging 300 homes. It demolished at least twenty homes to nothing. Thankfully, John, Deb, and the girls were safe. This was another difficult situation for John and Deb to face; there had been so many other hard issues for them already.

On Monday morning we took a taxi to the airport and flew to Bahia Negra in the TAM plane (Transporte Aereo Militar). One of the missionaries met us at the port with a motorboat to take us to Puerta Diana, which is actually the location of the Chamacoco Indian village, a few kilometers from the military base of Bahia Negra.

I went to work on the translation checking, and Fred went to work with John to try to clean up the mess left by the tornado. They worked hard, trying to pound out the tin roofing enough that it could at least be used temporarily until other materials could be purchased and shipped to them upriver. I was spending eight hours a day checking the book of Mark in Chamacoco.

One day while checking translation at Ulrich's, I heard little Jessica crying and screaming as if she was really hurt. She had stepped on a mandi'i fish in the river which has poison barbs. Deb said she has had adults cry with the pain. They put the stun gun on Jessica's foot, which alleviated the pain; the swelling went down immediately. It's interesting how that works. When I went over to the house later, Jessica was relaxed and napping.

Deb had several medical cases on a Sunday while we were there. Early in the morning, there was a young child with diarrhea; later, a bad knife wound mid-day from the previous night's drunken fight, and a bad head wound of a wife whose drunk husband hit her very hard with firewood and cracked her head open. Later someone brought a baby with pneumonia. Deb made no complaints. She just took care of everyone. John helped her with the woman's bad head wound. He did something I had never seen done before—he braided the woman's hair together to pull the wound closed. It worked.

Fred worked on the station's motor, which wasn't working when we got there. John and Deb's ham radio blew out, and the sewing machine was broken. Fred did fix the sewing machine to at least sew a straight stitch. The other co-worker had something wrong with her stove. There were so many disappointing things happening for various ones on the station. I went back to the room we were staying in at Ulrich's house to pray—and to be out of the way

After the translation check was completed, I went over to Deb's to help. As I was scrubbing the kitchen cupboard doors, prior to their being painted, Jessica came along wanting to help. She kept saying, "It's easier if someone works with you and helps you. I love my grandma, and I want to help her." She was so cute! She was four years old then. She told me two stories, reading *pictures* of two books the kids have. I helped Heather Dawn a couple mornings with her home-school studies prior to the plane coming to take us out.

A few days after returning to San Carlos we got news by mission radio that Bahía Negra had a storm with strong winds again, and part of the office roof (a building away from the house) of one of the other missionaries was taken off. John VA hadn't yet fixed the shutter on their bedroom from the last bad storm, so water got in there again.

Though these kinds of problems take place all over the world at any given time and seem so irrelevant in light of what other people suffer, they are things that can bring discouragement to the missionary as they experience the "when it rains, it pours" cycle. It's generally not just one difficult incident that knocks out some people from staying in the work; it's usually a buildup of several things—and just one more thing seems to be *the last straw that breaks the camel's back.*

During truly difficult times, when we might question if we are where we belong, it is important to know assuredly that we are in the place God wants us to be and that HE is sufficient to carry us through any crisis. Nothing comes to us that hasn't passed through His hands first. And whatever we may be feeling in a crisis, we can know He is present with us. Either His Word is true, or it isn't. And we have chosen to believe Him when He says, "I am with you even unto the end of the world."

*****

Spiritual Ministry vs. Physical Ministry? Where LAYS the Balance?

One hurdle that is difficult for some missionaries to conquer is the idea that some activities of missionary work are spiritual, and other areas are purely physical, or less spiritual. May I say right off that it is wrong to allow the physical, economical issues and the needs of the people to negate the teaching and preaching of God's Word (the main purpose for which we have gone to reach the indigenous people group), but it is also wrong to think it is unspiritual to be involved in helping, as needed, in the physical areas of the indigenous people's lives. As we show care and concern for their physical needs, they are more apt to listen to our message—recognizing that we love them and care for them as *whole* people.

I have heard an occasional person say, "I came here to preach the gospel; I didn't come here to help in the physical areas of the work."

I may be trained as a linguist, a Bible translator, a nurse, or have the spiritual gift of teaching—but does that mean I can't help in other physical areas when needed? Am I willing to be a "backup" for a missionary on furlough in a capacity that is not my favorite thing to do? Would I rather that an already overloaded co-worker take on more, while I stand by and say, "Don't ask me; I have my own job to do"?

There will be times when we need to cover one another's responsibilities to see the work go ahead smoothly. Not only do team members go on furlough, but they sometimes get sick and have to leave the work unexpectedly—hopefully only temporarily; or something else happens that takes them from the work for a time.

I oversaw the community store one year, while another co-worker was on furlough. Had I not done that, Fred would have had to do so—and he needed time for preparing lessons for the teaching of God's Word. Some were surprised I would do that; it wasn't a glamorous job at all, but it was an opportunity to show the people I cared for them.

"A team doesn't win the championship if its players are working from different agendas."
—John C. Maxwell

It takes time to train indigenous personnel to take over some of the areas that are needful to the community. Thankfully, not in every place that missionaries go to minister do they have to deal with such things, but among indigenous tribal people it's very common—especially when they are in isolated areas, having come from nomadic or semi-nomadic backgrounds.

We must not underestimate the influence we may have in the lives of individuals with whom we work in the *nitty-gritty* everyday work world—whatever the particular work may entail. The indigenous young man with whom I worked in the store became a very special friend to both Fred and me. He was in our home frequently; and after he married we had an opportunity to mentor him and his wife, along with a few other young couples. Later on, when he showed an interest in the medical field, I took him along to help treat the sick when I was medical backup. He is presently a trained nurse among his own people. The story of how that came to be will be given later on.

I taught a mid-week Angaite women's Bible class to relieve pressure from another co-worker who was feeling the pressure of an already "full plate," though teaching is not my thing; and I found it to be pressure myself. I never taught without preparing printed lessons to hand out to those present, which made my preparation time even more time-consuming. And when that co-worker was on furlough or off the station for other reasons, I was her backup Sunday School teacher for the women and girls. Again, I insisted on having printed lessons and tried to prepare two weeks in advance, as I was so afraid of not being prepared on time.

What I'm saying is that sometimes we are called upon to fill slots in which we are not particularly gifted. It certainly wasn't among my *spiritual gifts* according to any tests I took. And the fact that I had to put forth so much effort to do it is another clue that it wasn't my gift. Did God use the teaching anyway? I believe He did; He can work in spite of our weaknesses. And the fact that I had printed lessons, which the women saved and took home, bore fruit too, as some of the husbands who were fluent readers read those lessons and appreciated them. I found that out as they came to me asking for their own copies on occasion.

Why did I teach if it wasn't my gift? I was more fluent at the time in the language than others left on the station, so it fell to me to be the backup for the regular Sunday School teacher when she was gone. Once there were Angaite pastors teaching effectively, we dropped some of the women's classes, encouraging them to attend the classes their own people were teaching. But that didn't happen in a hurry.

It wasn't as difficult for me to work on other people's printed lessons for *them* to teach. I just wasn't comfortable doing the teaching myself. Fred wrote up his own lessons to teach, but he didn't always do them in Guarani. When he did do them in Guarani, he gave them to me to check and to print for his classes. Sometimes he did them in English for lack of time and gave them to me to translate for him—which could take many hours of preparation also. Anything I translated I always had a native speaker check to be sure it was correct and clearly understood.

We were blessed with having space for an office with the addition we put on—and we had good equipment with which to work for both school and church related materials, thanks to our teammates being willing to go together to finance some of the station equipment.

When someone needed to step up and take over the directorship of the Indian school, I saw the opportunity to build into those young teachers' lives and took on the responsibility, even though I had enough work already to warrant saying "no" to it. Again, I saw the potential that was there in those young men's lives and the opportunity for Fred and me to work together with them, their wives, and their families. They became leaders in the Angaite church.

As director of the school, the supervisor of Indian Schools in the capital city required me to spend a minimum of ninety hours during the teachers' summer vacation, further training them in their job responsibilities and weak areas. Although I saw the need for it, it was a lot of work for me (and the teachers). But I knew it was important that those teachers be qualified to do their jobs properly, or they could lose those jobs. It was because they had steady employment with the government that they were able to remain in the colony and not have to go look for work consistently like so many others. In that they were being trained to take leadership in the church, it meant the church wouldn't be left without faithful leadership present.

When it was obvious that they had an interest in the church music, but couldn't sing on tune with the guitar one of them was attempting to play, I offered to help. It was many hours of hard work, but it paid off. They, in turn, spent time with many of the young people, singing together in the evenings and on weekends to keep them from joining the drinking and dances that took place among the unbelievers.

While not everyone thought it important to spend so much time with the Indians on their music, I felt if it was important to them, it was important for someone to help them do well at it; and it was a good substitute for those things they had engaged in as unbelievers, which no longer held their interest. Many new songs were written for their use, and other instruments were introduced for their enjoyment. As music had always been a big part of my life, I realized how it could meet needs in the lives of these people, too. They were grateful for the help. It meant we often had young people in our living room in the evenings playing instruments— sometimes playing on their own, sometimes with me playing or working with them.

The hard thing about making close friendships among the people is that it is much harder when you have to leave the work for whatever reason. When they go through difficult times or trip and fall into sin, you feel torn and hurt with them as though they were your own kids. The blessing, however, of such a relationship was that they expected and accepted our involvement in their lives at times like that as well. They knew we loved them, and we had earned the right to deal with issues that came up if they weren't walking with the Lord as they ought. Our lives were enriched because of our relationship with them.

My personal mission statement written in my journal of May 1994, looks like this:

First Things
- A meaningful walk and relationship with the Lord.
- A meaningful, positive influence with husband, children, grandchildren, co-workers, neighbors, other family members, other missionaries in whose lives God might choose to use me. To be an encourager and positive motivator with people in my own sphere by my own example, in prayer for them, and giving *valid* helps.
- A meaningful influence in the lives of the Angaite people—leaving them something permanent (God's Word, teaching aids, etc.) in print, whereby they have opportunity to grow and develop spiritually.
- Personal development in adjusting socially wherever placed.

Roles and Goals
- Personal development: (time with God; continued education/study, exercise, relax?)
- Family relationships: (wife, mother, grandmother, sister, daughter, etc.)
- Co-worker/neighbor/friend: (fellow-missionaries and Indians.)
- Consultant: (encourager; includes language/translation helps)
- Secretary: (personal correspondence; JS's translation materials, etc.)
- Translation helper/checker: (help JS; check MU).
- Teacher: (Angaite ladies' class)

Long-Range Goals
- Help see Angaite translation project to completion; literacy program, new songbook, pedagogical grammar.
- Master's degree in social services (for ideas and understanding of varied cultures; to better interact and help others help themselves; to use my gift of *mercy* and gift of *exhortation* in proper balance.)

I didn't get to see the Angaite translation project to completion; the translator was moved to a different location where the people were still using their language freely, and he is still working on it. I did receive a master's degree in social services in June 1997, and a doctorate of education in missiology in November 1999, from Lael College and Graduate School. Mention will be made later as to how those degrees were helpful in helping others get needed training. Getting a college education by extension was not easy. It meant evening study, when and if there was opportunity for such without neglecting other responsibilities; it was long and drawn out for lack of finances to get it done sooner.

Mention is made of the various areas in which I got involved, or assignments I was asked to do, to show that it doesn't pay to have preconceived ideas of what you will or will not do on the mission field. God delights to use us many times in spite of our weaknesses.

Occasionally my co-workers came with ideas and assignments of things they wanted me to do—like translate a booklet on eternal security (which I did), AWANA verse booklets for the children's AWANA program, special letters for their supporters, etc. The schoolteachers were always arriving with more requests (*last minute*).

I wrote up a booklet on goal setting for missionary wives and mothers and a small booklet on attitudes after reading John Maxwell's book *Your Attitude, Key to Success* to share with some of the missionary women on our field. These were the kind of projects I enjoyed doing. Although work was involved in making a nice booklet, it was relaxing and fun to see the finished product.

The new field director asked me to make up a handbook on language and culture for the missionaries' language study purposes, which was a big project. It was not an easy assignment. For any book or booklet I made, I always did the cover first. That was the fun part. I would then leave it out on my desk, where I could see it to keep me motivated to complete the book.

If you were to read my journals during those years at San Carlos, you would see several entries that read something like this one: "The polverine [no seeums] are biting like crazy this a.m.; it's hard to sit still. Though I have on long pants and a long-sleeved shirt, the back of my neck, ears, hands, and face are really being bit. They get behind one's glasses and anywhere the skin isn't covered. They are awful little creatures, making me feel like I'm on fire."

We contended with mosquitoes and chiggers as well. The biting bugs, along with intense heat and high humidity, could make a person feel irritable and edgy. Good praise music on in the background was helpful in keeping a right focus and remembering why we were there.

In February 1994, John, Deb and the two girls left the field. It was hard to see them leave. We missed them terribly. John was having some physical problems that turned into depression, developing into spiritual problems; they felt they needed to make a change and returned to the States. We love them dearly and were so sad to see them leave. They were very much loved by the Chamacoco people with whom they worked.

Certainly none of us are exempt from facing and experiencing spiritual battles as we step out in faith to serve the Lord—desiring that our lives bring glory to Him. It's a *given* that the enemy will do all he can to discourage us and try to see us removed from the ministry in which we are involved.

*****

On February 12, 1994, Joshua Caleb Sammons was born to Dave and Tammy. Josh is our twelfth grandchild and the last. We now await the *great-grands*.

The difficulties of life are intended to make us better — not bitter.

19
MARXIST AGITATION

It was while we were on home assignment in 1997 that the president of the colony (an unsaved man) was contacted by a Liberation Theology priest who told him he knew of an organization (recently formed) that could help them, but they needed to get rid of the missionaries to get that help. That priest had already caused division among the Paraguayan nationals in the area in which he lived, telling the poor people it was okay to steal cattle and other things from the schoolteachers in the area, who had worked hard for what they had.

The men who represented the organization mentioned were all Paraguayans, most of them young lawyers or anthropologists (or both), who had gone to Europe for their training. They came back to "help" the poor country people and the indigenous people fight for their *rights*. They mostly led demonstrations against the government and caused a lot of division everywhere they went—causing division among the Indians as well.

Although some of what they said was true, they used a little bit of truth mixed with a lot of lies to sway the people to their way of thinking. They made promises of free food, tools, clothing, blankets, and so on. They did supply some of these things every once in a great while just to keep the people on the hook—the people believing they were going to be better off by choosing to follow this group. But each time the indigenous people took off to Asunción to demonstrate against the government, it meant their gardens were left uncared for; they left any work they may have had for neighboring ranchers (as the Marxists turned them against those individuals also), making them worse off than they had been previously.

The Indians were encouraged by the Marxist group to return to their old ways of living, meaning the shamanism (witchcraft), drinking, and dancing that had caused so many breakups before in families. They talked out of both sides of their mouths at once, and many of the people didn't seem to see through that. At one moment they said they were to return to the shamans/witchdoctors for medicine, criticizing the missionary for bringing in modern medicines. At the same time, they were asking the people to demonstrate against the government for not having sufficient medical help.

They actually had people lie on a tape recording against the missionaries, against the colony school, and against the teachers, then played it on the national radio for all to hear. The people who spoke on tape didn't even have children in the school—but who was to know that unless they lived at San Carlos? It was very stressful. Those lawyers lied about a lot of things and got others to lie. What benefits the indigenous people got for lying, I do not know. But those lawyers told the schoolteachers they would one day be very sorry for following the missionaries' beliefs. They didn't like it when some of the things they propagated were questioned by the schoolteachers of the colony—with whom we had spent a lot of time mentoring, and who seemingly had confidence in our word. Though the teachers were not against their people getting help, they began to recognize the double talk and had questions.

The opposition group did everything they could to try to ruin the school and the teachers. With the help of the radicals, they even started another school at the opposite end of the village, and they brought in a Paraguayan schoolteacher to teach. I don't know if that school still operates today or not, and if so, how it is going—but when we were there, the teacher wasn't even present much of the time. She taught in Spanish, which none of the children understood; we were told they didn't seem to be learning at all. It was mostly an attempt to ruin the school we had developed, which had been progressing well up to the time we left. They were trying to ruin the three indigenous teachers because they were strong believers and leaders in the church. Some parents who had removed their kids from the school we had developed because of pressure from the opposition, later sent their kids back to the school, recognizing they got a better education there.

The lawyers and anthropologists behind the opposition were constantly visiting the colony, having meetings with the people to tell them they needed to kick us off the property. They told the Indians we were taking from them, and that we were using finances that were given for them, all of which was false. There may have been organizations that raised money for poor people and pocketed it for themselves—but it certainly wasn't the missionaries; those lawyers had ways to know that what they were saying was untrue. There was even a radio station that was connected to this type of thinking, and they propagated lies continually.

After all that the missionaries had done for the people over the years, it was hard to understand how any of them could believe those lies. Not everyone believed them—but enough of them were wanting a free handout that they would believe anything to get what they wanted. It was causing division throughout the village. Families were becoming divided on the issue. It was sad. Most of them didn't even realize what the real reason behind the opposition was. They were just following the crowd, not knowing what they were following.

Many of the people in the village were upset about what was happening and got together to vote in a new leader for the colony; a majority of the people joined them. But the previous leader refused to back down, and he went to the Marxist group for help. Through pulling strings and a lot of crookedness, they managed to keep him as a leader—but the government Indian department also recognized the group who had chosen a new leader. Thus, the colony was divided politically, causing for a lot of animosity between the two groups for quite a while. Most of the people didn't even understand what all was involved, except that they were going to get free help. And who going through hard times wouldn't welcome such! The sad part is, I don't think the radical organization even cared that much about the Indians and their future. They were just using them to serve their own cause.

It was getting harder for the missionaries to function in the colony, and it was decided by our field leadership that some of the team should begin phasing out, which they did. There were just two of us left—another family and us—to phase out a bit later.

When we knew the mission was planning to phase out of San Carlos, only visiting on an itinerant basis, we updated all the school textbooks and printed them—sending them to town to have hardback covers so they would last much longer. Previously the books were spiraled and had workbook sections included. Once we made more permanent textbooks, the workbooks were either separate, or answers had to be written only in the students' notebooks and handed in to the teacher. There would be no more writing answers in the textbooks.

It was becoming obvious that our time in San Carlos as residents might be ending even sooner than we had planned. We wanted to be diligent in seeing that people were trained to carry on all aspects of the work when we were gone.

Though there were three teachers functioning in the school, only one of them was being paid by the government. He had been involved in the school for several years already, so I planned to get permission from the supervisor to train him as the new director of the school. The missionaries had been paying the other two teachers until we could get government pay for them. We put in applications for the other two teachers to get government pay, only to find out they did not have sixth-grade records on file nor could we find any such records at San Carlos.

I got permission to give exams to those two teachers so they could qualify for government pay, and I sent their grades in to the supervisor. It took a long time and many hassles before they actually received pay from the government, but it did happen before we had to leave the colony. Thanks to much prayer, along with the help of a friend in government who went to bat for us (recognizing my credentials and recommendation), the teachers were finally recognized.

The other missionary couple spent time teaching first aid to a few interested individuals in the hope that they could better help their own people. Not all those who had shown an interest were actually adept at taking on such a responsibility, but a couple of them did quite well—one of them being David Álvarez, whom I had also taught in a class with the schoolteachers, using *Where There is No Doctor* (in Spanish) as the main textbook. I contacted the hospital in Concepción and made friends with some medical personnel there, who agreed to do what they could to help David learn more so he could become a health promoter in his village.

David had been helping with the vaccination program at San Carlos, and the hospital personnel were impressed with his abilities and interest. Thus, the specialist in charge of leprosy and tuberculosis sent him to a Mennonite hospital to train in the lab to recognize both leprosy and tuberculosis. There were many leprosy and TB patients there. We only knew there to be three cases of leprosy in San Carlos, but there was a lot of tuberculosis.

David, having helped me in the medical work and wanting to get further medical training to help his own people, had never finished sixth-grade—though he had spent two years in the Paraguayan military. I told him he would never be able to get into any health promotion program without completing the sixth-grade, and he could take it under me if he did so right away before I turned over the directorship to Carlos, the more experienced school teacher. David did complete the exams and had his sixth-grade certificate before we left the station.

When it was decided that we would have to move from San Carlos, we talked with our field leadership and got permission to move to Concepción, a small town downriver. We wanted to be close enough to still be of help and encouragement to the Angaite pastors and teachers. The schoolteachers pay hadn't yet been shifted to Concepción where the teachers could go by boat to collect it themselves on a monthly basis. Everything had previously been done in the capital city of Asunción; the mission administrator kindly took care of it and sent the money on to the teachers. We had tried for a long time to get their pay switched to Concepción, and it finally happened—but anything like that with the government is slow to take place.

Fred and I had gone to Concepción a couple of times to try to find a place to rent. Anything that seemed decent was expensive; given the fact that we were Americans, the Paraguayans figured we were rich and wanted to charge high rent compared to what others paid in the area. We couldn't rent anything in an isolated area either, having to keep in mind we needed to be in a secure location as Americans. There had been several kidnappings in recent days, and New Tribes Mission had already lost other missionaries, who had been kidnapped and killed in other countries.

We finally found a large, commercial-type building right on a main street in the middle of other businesses that was for rent and had been empty for quite a while. The last renter had been killed inside the place, and people were superstitious about living in it. It was big and ugly, but it looked like a safe place to live (once we made the windows and doors more secure). It was a price we could afford to pay ($135.00/month); so we paid down something to secure it and went off to our annual field conference with plans to move in afterwards. Our Angaite friends were happy to know we would be where they could contact us, if need be; David Álvarez planned to stay with us when coming to town to get the vaccinations for San Carlos.

We had a surprise awaiting us in Asunción that was totally unexpected and somewhat upsetting. The field director who had replaced Fred was already gone to work on the stateside end, and Pete was now the acting field director. His assistant, who was to be groomed to take his place while he went on furlough, had to leave the field because of an eye problem his wife needed to have taken care of by a specialist; the doctor in Paraguay felt they should go to the United States. Pete was asking us to move to Asunción for Fred to be acting field director until he returned from furlough. I voted against it, but everyone else was voting for it.

Fred and I spent a good deal of time in prayer and talking with one another, as we had promised the Angaite we would be available to them; we knew they still needed help and encouragement on a regular basis. We felt that to break our word would be bad with the situation as it was. So, with more talking the situation over with Pete and the remaining Asunción staff, a "win-win" agreement was made. Fred would divide his time between Asunción and Concepción for the year. It may not have been the best arrangement, but it worked. I went with him to Asunción until some unexpected changes in our lives took place.

20
LIFE IN CONCEPCION

2002 – June 2005

Serving the Lord in Concepción, Paraguay

Developing Biblical studies in Guarani

Fred & Ruthie Sammons

Headquarters:
New Tribes Mission
1000 E. First St.
Sanford, FL 32771

Mailing Address:
Fred & Ruthie Sammons
Casilla 1181
Asunción, Paraguay

e-mail: fred_sammons@ntm.org

Faith cometh by hearing and hearing by the Word of God

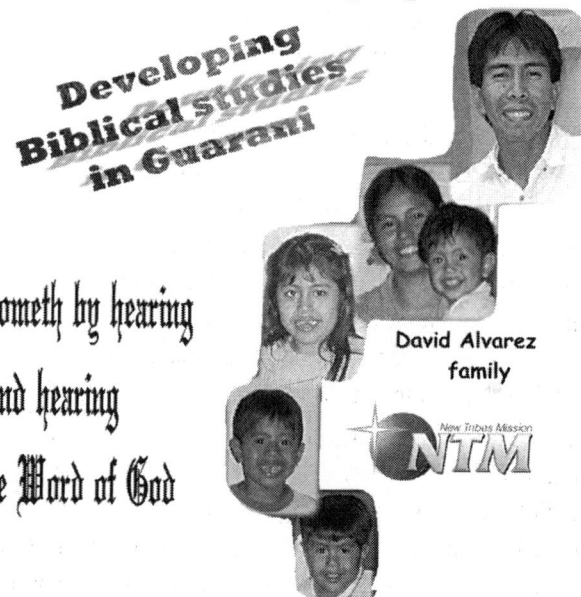

David Alvarez family

NTM

The above was a prayer card we gave out asking for prayer. We were still developing Biblical studies in Guarani while living in Concepción.

After attending the mission conference we returned to Concepción to check over the place we had just rented, and we purchased a few items to get started and did some painting. We then made a trip back to San Carlos to get the rest of our belongings and move them to Concepción by a cattle boat. So, ugly and big as the house was, we were glad to have it. We did a lot of work, cleaning, painting, and repairing. There was a bathroom upstairs with running water, but no water downstairs, except outside in a very ugly, rundown sort of kitchen, which we turned into a storage area and workshop for Fred. Fred piped in water downstairs to make an inside kitchen. He found out the electricity in the place wasn't wired properly, and he corrected that. The place wasn't what you could call beautiful, but it was certainly livable, and we appreciated it. We had lived in Concepción only a few months when our lives took a big change we never anticipated.

The hospital personnel in Concepción had previously asked us if we would please keep up the vaccination program at San Carlos, even though we were no longer living on the colony. So I had been helping David Alvarez keep up the vaccinations, and David took the responsibility of filling out the paperwork as volunteer health promoter. This would give David contact with the hospital personnel, and he would be able to carry on the work later on when we would no longer be available. We set up a room for David to stay in when he would come for vaccines.

The hospital personnel in charge of vaccination records were very impressed with David, as was the medical specialist in leprosy and tuberculosis. He took a real liking to David and suggested he get some nurses' training there in Concepción. But David had a wife and three children at the time, expecting a fourth child soon.

At the time this suggestion was made to David, it just happened that our son Steve had come to Paraguay to visit briefly, bringing his teenage daughter Janelle with him. Janelle wanted to see the Iguazu Falls, so Fred took her to the Falls, and Steve went with me to Concepción to meet David Álvarez, who would be arriving there on business. We only had one day together there, but that day changed our lives—and David's.

Steve hadn't had occasion to speak the Guarani language for many years, but he was very fluent in Spanish; so I told David to expect Steve to talk to him in Spanish—but that he would probably understand David's Guarani. As soon as the two met, and David spoke to Steve in Guarani, Steve responded in Guarani. Later, when Steve wasn't around, David said to me, "I thought you said Steve didn't speak Guarani; he speaks fine."

David had been to the hospital on business and had checked about the nursing school, and found out they required a minimum of a ninth grade education to enter that course. Remember he had just recently finished sixth-grade with me—already being in his twenties. Previously, they had allowed health promoters who worked in the interior to train after completing sixth-grade, but that option was no longer available. They had previously allowed the person to come to town to study for a week or ten days a month, then return home, to continue the same way on a routine basis. But that option no longer existed either.

Thanks to Steve's understanding Guarani, when David told me that one of the medical people at the hospital told him there was an Institute there in town where he could take rapid courses to finish through ninth grade, Steve spoke up and said:, "Go for it." I said, "Steve, he can't do that. He has a wife and three kids with a fourth one due soon. He can't leave them to come here to go to school. He has to take care of his family." Steve said, "You have a big house." Then he looked at David and said, "Come live with Mom."

David and I just looked at each other. Neither of us ever had such a thought before. We hadn't had children living in our home for over twenty years, and more like thirty-some years for little ones. However, Fred and I both felt the medical work in San Carlos was important and that no one was sufficiently trained to do it. We talked it over, prayed about it and felt that God would have us to take in the Álvarez family to live with us for David to go to school.

Now we knew why God allowed us to have that big house. It wasn't too big for a family of eight; it was perfect. Although we didn't know we would need all that space, God knew.

So, in July 2002, David and his family moved in with us as one big happy family. We went up to San Carlos to help them move down with us. I asked a neighboring rancher friend up there who had a motorboat if we could hire him to take Celinda, the children, and me to Concepción; I didn't think it would be good for Celinda to take the long boat ride downriver in her condition, as it appeared the baby was due soon. Fred and David would take the slow boat downriver. We arrived in Concepción on a Friday afternoon, and that baby was born the following night at midnight. David was only there a few hours before the baby was born. The baby was home with us twelve hours later, and the parents told me I could name him.

I named that little baby Esteban Pablo for our Steve, whose name is Stephen Paul, as it was his idea that this family move in with us. That little boy became very special to us; it was hard to leave him. He thought we were his real grandparents; after we were gone he wondered why we never went to see them anymore.

David and Celinda's first child was named Ruthy, after me. I had the privilege of being with Celinda when little Ruthy was born. Normally those people didn't bother to name their children for weeks, sometimes months. But she was named the day she was born.

When David and Celinda moved in, the kids were baby Esteban (born the day after the family moved in), two-year-old Crispín, four-year-old Cristian, and five-year-old Ruthy. Ruthy turned six just a couple months later. We enrolled her in kindergarten at the Presbyterian school (even though it was time for their second semester), because she did not know any Spanish, and that would give her a chance to acquire some Spanish before the following school year. There were no other indigenous children in the school, so that was an adjustment. We purposefully chose the Presbyterian school over the public school, as we knew she would be treated better there, at least by the staff. She then took the full year of kindergarten the next year. In 2004 she entered first grade, and we enrolled Cristian into the kindergarten program.

This *added project* (with the Álvarez family living with us) was not part of our assigned mission work, so we had to continue carrying on all previous work besides having the family to care for and to help in their schooling. This didn't affect Fred as much as it did me—though he might challenge that statement because he didn't have *me* all to himself. Fred continued to travel, study, work on Bible lessons and carry on all his normal responsibilities; I continued in consultant work and translation projects, as well as overseeing David's schooling and continuing work on some more permanent textbooks for the San Carlos school.

This picture was taken in December 2004, of us with the Álvarez family.

The Álvarez family had many medical and dental expenses while living with us; they had no way to financially take care of those expenses, of course. Though we lived and ate simply, finances were often tight because our household and living expenses more than doubled with the addition of six more people to care for. Not only did David and Celinda have a lot of needed dental work, but the two older children had mouths full of rotten teeth from being malnourished as babies. The younger two had better teeth because we saw that Celinda had prenatal pills while carrying those babies, and they were better fed while living with us. We insisted they eat good food before having sweets, extra bread, etc.—things kids prefer to eat.

It was initially a big adjustment to have four little ones in the house after many years of having no children at home at all; and two adult women under the same roof wasn't always easy either. Amazingly, we had very few confrontations over the period of three years living together—that, I believe, was quite an accomplishment.

DAVID'S SCHOOLING:

We got David enrolled at the Institute del Norte in Concepción, and I enrolled with him in seventh-grade night school. He studied at home all day and attended classes at night. Because he did not speak Spanish I went to school with him so I could better help him at home with his studies. After he finished seventh grade I went with him to eighth grade just for math and Spanish classes, again helping him at home as necessary during the day.

When David enrolled in ninth grade I no longer went to class with him. He was one month away from finishing ninth grade when we found out that the requirements of the nursing school had changed from having a ninth-grade certificate to a twelfth-grade diploma. *Now what?* That was October 2003, and Fred said we were leaving Paraguay by June 2005, regardless. He would be seventy years old, and the mission was now asking the missionaries to retire at age seventy. Wow! What to do next?

Our son Steve had encouraged me years ago to study by correspondence and get a college degree perchance the day would come that I would want to teach somewhere where a degree was required. I never had a desire to teach publicly. I have enjoyed helping those who need special help because they are committed to a worthy goal that would be difficult to reach without the special help. And in the case of helping train the indigenous school teachers and David, their reason to study was to help their community, not just for their own personal benefit, so I found helping them very fulfilling.

When we heard David needed to finish twelfth grade to be able to enter the nursing school, I talked to the Spanish teacher David had for grades 7-9. I asked her if she had any ideas of what we could do. She said, "Teach him yourself. You have your doctor's degree. Get him the texts he needs, have him study them; then when he's ready, you make application with the Ministry of Education in Asunción for him to take his final exams at a school here in Concepción that Asunción recognizes." It sounded overwhelmingly complicated to me.

How could I possibly teach him three years of high school and get him enrolled in the nursing course—all to be completed within a year and a half?

First I talked to David and Celinda to ask if they were willing to make the sacrifice and commitment it was going to take to complete such a goal. *I'm sure they had no idea just how hard it was going to be.* I stressed that it would be a sacrifice on the part of all of us in the family, but I was willing to do my part if they were ready to do theirs. We had invested so much already, I didn't want to quit without at least trying to fulfill that goal.

No one (except that Spanish teacher) was very supportive of the fact it could be done. My own daughter said, "Mom, what are you thinking? You're going to drive that kid nuts and yourself as well." But I just couldn't believe God would bring us this far to have us abandon the project, and David felt the same. Fred was supportive; he just continued to state that it had to be completed in the time frame mentioned, as we weren't staying years longer just to get David through school.

I went to the director of nursing to ask her permission for David to enter the nursing school with the promise that I would see he finished grade 12 before nursing graduation, but she said she wasn't the one who could give that permission. She knew David from his contact with the hospital and liked him, and she was willing to give him a chance; but she could not make the decision. She told me the person to contact in Asunción who would have to allow that exception, as the potential students were not allowed to even take the entrance exam without permission from the Ministry of Health in Asunción; that permission was given only after they saw all the students' paperwork—meaning their title of having finished twelfth grade.

I sent letters to the doctors in charge of the proper department to make that decision and I got an interview with the vice-minister of education and culture in Asunción through a friend, who was his sub-secretary. When he saw my credentials, he was willing to at least speak for me to the "powers that be" in the health department.

To make a long story short, it took several phone calls and pursuing that situation before I could ever get the permission for David to enroll in the nursing program. No one believed he could possibly accomplish all that work in that period of time, but we had to try. Given the fact that David was *indigenous*, it was believed to be even more improbable that he was even qualified to do such.

I will not say there weren't difficult days. I still had mission work to keep up with besides running a household of eight and helping David besides. There were difficult days for David too. He studied high school subjects at home most days, going to nursing school at night. Sometimes he had to cancel one or the other to work on whichever exams were most pressing at the time. There were times, I'm sure, when he wondered if his head could hold any more information. And, believe me, by the time he finished, I felt like I had burned out *my* brain.

I went to one of the schools and got a list of all the texts needed for grades 10–12, gave the list to Fred, and he went to Asunción and bought all the textbooks.

I hired a tutor for advanced math and another tutor for physics and chemistry (young married men who came to the house to teach David). For the other seven subjects, I read the textbooks and summarized them for David into the computer and printed them out into booklet form for him to study. I copied the questions and answers for him as well. When it was time for his exams, I gave him three copies (per his request) of the printed questions without the answers so he could practice answering the questions and then check himself.

Fred and I insisted that David be in the office studying during certain hours; I know that discipline at times had to be hard because it was against everything he had been used to. It was hard for Celinda, too. Even though she had "break" times with him a couple hours after lunch, she wasn't used to being scheduled either. Celinda and I shared the housework, the cooking, cleaning, and so on; we had a smooth working system in that respect.

We had the expense of the family's food, their clothing, schooling, medical bills, dental bills, and whatever else they needed. We paid for all the trips back to San Carlos to do vaccinations, and we bought David a microscope to do lab work for TB and leprosy, as was suggested to us by the doctors after he studied at a Mennonite hospital. There were many expenses involved, but God was good and provided for us all. It meant living as simply as possible to make the finances stretch, but it was worth it.

We took on this project voluntarily, apart from our mission work, though we felt it every bit as important as our assigned mission work. We did not feel our job at San Carlos was really complete until we had helped to see a medical person trained to work on that station. It was a lot of work for all of us, but unbelievably, we completed it before the deadline—and not much ahead of it!

David took his family home early during his last semester of training so he would be free to study for finals; and we were getting ready to leave Paraguay soon after his graduation. His wife and some of his relatives came to attend his graduation and stayed the night at our house. It was a great day when graduation from the nursing class took place. David was valedictorian of his class. He was the first indigenous person to ever attend that school, and all our neighbors were as happy as we were when they heard the outcome of David's schooling. The director of nursing was so proud of David, as were all his teachers. At his graduation she said to us, "I know you came to Paraguay to minister to the people about God, but as far as I'm concerned you completed your mission when you put David through school. In the twenty-five years since this school began, David is the first indigenous person to enroll and to graduate. You have opened the door for others. It's time that happens."

David Álvarez graduated from the nursing program on Monday, June 6, 2005; he returned to San Carlos by boat the next day.

Here, at the request of the hospital, David Álvarez is taking a census of the Angaite people living in a village at the edge of town in Concepción.

It was more than a year after David received his title from the nursing school that he was officially recognized as an employee of the Ministry of Health in Asunción and able to work as a health promoter in his own colony with pay. He did do some work for the hospital off and on while he was waiting for his paperwork to go through, but that took him from his family and wasn't what he wanted to do on a permanent basis.

This was a tremendous accomplishment on David's part. In a July 2009 email from missionaries who had recently visited San Carlos, they said David was very busy with the medical work. They also sent a picture of his two older children, who were baptized that month. That is good news. David is a natural at caring for medical needs and very much liked by all the people in the colony, regardless of the political side they have chosen. He has made himself available to help anyone—even the Paraguayan neighbors. To keep his job with the health department means making application every year seemingly. We continue to pray daily for him and his family.

Here, David Álvarez is taking home his family to San Carlos from Concepción. David is at the front on that plank, boarding the boat with two of the boys; young Ruthy is between the parents; Celinda is carrying the youngest.

David with the bicycle we bought him as a graduation gift.

This picture was taken in November 2005. There have been many plants added since then, as well as pavers in the patio—for more pleasant outdoor entertaining.

This picture was taken a few years later.

21
MOVE TO THE USA

David Álvarez graduated from the nursing school on Monday, June 6; he left Concepción to return to San Carlos the next day. Wednesday evening, June 8, our Paraguayan neighbor women had a going-away tea for me at the hotel next-door. That was special. They said they would all miss us as neighbors; they even gave us some going away gifts, begging us to return to visit them and to try to keep in contact somehow. Obviously they had observed what was going on at our house while living there—from comments they made, which were all very kind. I have to admit that I was surprised at their going out of their way to show me such kindness. They were all strong Catholics. We had given all of them books that presented the gospel clearly and spoke to them of the Lord and what He meant to us when we had opportunity, but to our knowledge none of these had made a personal decision to accept Christ as their personal Savior. (The math tutor, whom I had hired to teach David advanced math, did write to us later about his decision to accept the Lord after reading the book we had left him—the same book we gave to all of David's teachers and to our neighbors.)

On Friday, June 10, we left Concepción. I walked through the house one last time in tears; I was going to miss this place. Amazing how you can adjust to the noise on the main street, along with everything else that seemed so annoying upon first moving in. It was the people, of course, that made the place special.

From June 13–15, I did my last translation check, checking the Gospel of John for the Wycliffe missionary who was now translating for the Maca people. My sister Alice was present to observe, as she would be taking my place after I left. It was a tearful parting with my sister on June 17, when they returned to their work interior with the Ayore. We appreciated Bruce and Alice so much; they were not only family but also special friends.

We left the airport of Asunción, Paraguay, on the afternoon of June 23, 2005. Jim, Dora, and their three younger sons were on the same plane until we reached Sao Paulo, Brazil. In Brazil we boarded separate planes—each headed to a different destination. They were on their way to Florida to visit Jim's parents, then to Waukesha, Wisconsin, where their oldest son Danny was living at the time. We were on our way to San Diego, California, where our three other kids and their families were living.

We arrived in San Diego at 8:30 a.m. local time on June 24. Steve and his son Jason met us at the airport. We went to Steve and Monica's and saw our car (a 1997, two-door Toyota Rav 4), which Steve found for us on the internet. We had told him ahead of time how much we could spend on a car, and we asked him to watch for something for us. The car is perfect for us.

We had asked Dave to check around and see if he could find us a place we could afford to rent in Ramona so we could be close to the three families. It was decided we couldn't afford to live in Southern California unless we were satisfied to live in a Park Model RV on Dave and Tammy's property; by law they couldn't have an RV over 400 sq. feet on their property.

Though we could have gone to our mission's retirement center in Sanford, Florida, we chose to be near our kids and grandkids. We're glad we made that choice.

Steve and Dave cleared and leveled the area for the trailer. Dave had worked very hard on the landscaping around it, and he made a freestanding deck up against it. Though it is much less space than we were used to, we've managed well with it; and in time, Fred and Dave added a shed nearby, which doubles for storage, laundry room, and Fred's office.

So what is it like returning to the United States to live after so many years in South America? I have to admit it was total culture shock for me. So many things were different than I expected them to be. I just didn't feel like I "fit" anywhere. I shed many tears those first months back—seemingly without any good reason. I wasn't sure myself why I was feeling so "out of it." I had every reason to be grateful for a nice place to live and able to be close to our kids. It's difficult to explain how anyone would find that hard to adjust to, but everything I knew and had been involved in over the years was all of a sudden gone, and I didn't seem to know how to "fit" into the situation here. Our daughter Deb was a big help, as she had been through the same things already years earlier. She was very understanding and called frequently to encourage me.

The mission sent us a book to read, *Coming Home*, stressing the need to be careful to not be critical toward the changes we would find since having been gone, and to keep in mind that *we too* have changed after living in another culture for so many years.

I don't believe the adjustment was as hard for Fred as it was for me. He had looked forward to retirement and change. Although he probably missed some of the ministry he was in, he has since become involved in a men's Bible study group that has made a big difference for him as well as leading a "home group" Bible study.

The first time I went grocery shopping I ended up in tears; I told Fred, "There is no way we can afford to live here." Everything was so expensive. And, our vehicle in Concepción was a motorbike, and it certainly was more economical to run than a car. There were so many things to think about—finding a doctor and dentist and discovering that medical expenses here were so much more than they had been in Paraguay. But God had taken care of us all these many years; He wasn't about to abandon us now. I knew things would work out one way or another, but that didn't take away the fact that it was a big adjustment to make. I needed to see it as new opportunities and to trust that God knew what He was doing and wanted to do in our lives.

In 2006, I had the privilege of translating into Spanish a manual for Overcomers in Christ (an organization that works with people recovering from addictions; their headquarters is located in Omaha, Nebraska) The work was done on a volunteer basis and took the first six months of 2006. In 2007 they asked for some revision to match their 2007 English manual. I finally felt I was doing something that was within my gift-bag to do.

I worked as a volunteer counselor for the Ramona Pregnancy Care Clinic twice a week for one year, then dropped to just a couple times a month because of other activities and responsibilities. Occasionally I have translated something for them, as they have many Hispanic clients, some who don't speak English. I did checking by email for one of the missionaries in Paraguay (in Guarani) for a time, but that has been finished, and that missionary has recently retired.

As we have become involved in church home groups, we have made friends and are now feeling like we belong here. I can't say I have totally found my "niche" yet, but I think I may be getting there, little by little. I am often reminded of the fact that this world is not our home, so it may not be so odd to feel like a foreigner and stranger at times.

It has definitely been a blessing to be close to our adult kids, and to have the opportunity to become better acquainted with our grandchildren. We miss the ones in Wisconsin, but Jim and Dora are now happily serving in the New Tribes Bible Institute in Waukesha, involved in the lives of the students there, discipling them and seeing them trained for the Lord's work wherever He chooses to use them. Dora is one of the deans of women, and Jim is on the educational staff.

Do I miss Paraguay? I miss some of the people there and not being able to keep in contact with those we worked with for so long—to know how they are doing physically and spiritually. Because the mission has *phased out* of that work (except for occasional itinerant visits), we know very little of what is really going on in that village.

And, life in Southern California? I know why our three kids who live out here are content to stay here, regardless of how difficult it sometimes has been for them financially. San Diego County is a great place to live for those people who love variety—the beach, the desert, the ocean or the mountains. And this is horse country for those who love horses. (None of our family members have horses, but the neighbors do.) For those of us not interested in those things, we enjoy the mild climate. I'm here for family—but definitely appreciate the climate.

It's true that California has fires and earthquakes. We did have to evacuate in October 2007 for a week because of the fires, but thankfully Steve and Monica lived just far enough away from the fire that we were safe there. Weather-wise, it's not so different living here than it was in Paraguay. There aren't as many bugs here—few mosquitoes and no polverine. *That's* a blessing!

And one couldn't beat the view where we live. If only you could come sit with me in our outside patio and quietly watch so much of God's wonderful creation. The day I was sitting outside writing this chapter, I observed the following: a small black-and-white woodpecker was pecking away at the base of the large oak tree nearby; sparrows were fighting over the seeds in a hanging bird feeder; a dozen finch were eating away on the finch sock; and a flock of quail were eating cracked corn, as well as seed that the other birds were dropping.

A couple of gorgeous blue jays were flitting around, vying for the sunflower seeds in a hanging basket, as a red-throated hummingbird flit from flower to flower or drank at the hummingbird feeder. It's fun to see the occasional roadrunners that cross the yard but won't stick around when they see us. Normally there's a squirrel or two eating cracked corn along with the birds, and an occasional rabbit. The rabbits, though cute, are a nuisance because of being so destructive to plants and grass. (The gophers are bad news, too.)

In fewer numbers (but seen from time to time, scaring away everything else temporarily), have been owls, vultures, crows, a fox or a coyote—and even a bobcat or mountain lion.

[We had to quit feeding the birds later on when we realized the seed was attracting the rats and the squirrels. The rats got into the wall of the trailer and chewed the electric wires, which caused a short, and burned out many appliances.]

What a perfect spot to park our Park Model RV, right on our son Dave's property, where we not only enjoy the landscaping he did around our little place but where we see the beauty of his own yard with many lovely plants, flowers, and trees, with mountains in view in the background. To top it all off, you can't beat the neighbors! How many people are privileged to live that close to their married kids and grandkids?

As I watch the little birds, I am reminded of the scripture that says, *"Are not two sparrows sold for a penny? Yet not one of them will fall to the ground apart from the will of your Father. And even the very hairs of your head are all numbered. So don't be afraid; you are worth more than many sparrows."* (Matthew 10:30-31)

Also found in Luke: *"Are not five sparrows sold for two pennies? Yet not one of them is forgotten by God. Indeed, the very hairs of your head are all numbered. Don't be afraid; you are worth more than many sparrows."* (Luke 12:6-7)

God enjoys variety in all of His creation—we humans included. We are all precious to him, regardless of race, background, or personality. It's said that no two snowflakes are identical. Imagine! Billions of them, and no two alike. The same is true of us as human beings. God has uniquely designed each one of us—no two persons being exactly alike, and yet He loves each of us the same.

Does God have a plan and a purpose for each individual? He does. Mainly that purpose is for us who are believers and followers of Jesus Christ to live a Christ-like life, glorifying Him on this earth and discipling others for Him. But where and how God chooses to use us to do that will vary a great deal from one individual to another. May we show love and respect to one another as God's children, thankful for the fact that He has called each one of us to serve Him wherever we are.

Whether a follower of Jesus Christ is in a so-called full-time Christian ministry or is involved in a full-time lay occupation, his or her primary purpose in life should be to live an exemplary lifestyle that is pleasing to the Lord and that draws others to Christ. God alone knows where each of us can best do that; and He will give us wisdom and direction as we look to Him.

Because we believe God called us to a cross-cultural ministry to yet-unreached indigenous people, we joined New Tribes Mission whose main purpose for existence is to reach the unreached people groups around the world, and we served with them for forty-three years.

Having spent so many years away from our children and grandchildren, it is my desire to share with them some of our missionary experiences; maybe it will help explain why we walk to a different drumbeat. There is only one thing in life that is truly important and fulfilling, and that is to personally know God, to know His will—and then to do it.

We are grateful for the many years God allowed us to serve Him in Paraguay. We have never been sorry for the choice we made to follow the Lord into missionary work for which we felt He gifted us and called us to (Matthew 28:19–20). It was not without difficulties, disappointments and our share of mistakes, but we wouldn't change our life's calling for anything in the world. God is so good!

My prayer is that each one of our family—children and grandchildren—experience the joy that comes from an intimate relationship with the Lord, knowing God's purpose for their lives and seeing that purpose fulfilled in obedience to Him.

Our children have always been a great blessing to us. They shared in our ministry in Paraguay, always able to be with us when we lived in the interior—helping in the mission work and continuing their education through home-schooling. Now, it is a blessing to have opportunity to be near family during our retirement years. And as III John:4 says, *"I have no greater joy than to know my children walk in truth."*

Ruthy Álvarez is being baptized here by her two uncles, who are both pastors at San Carlos.

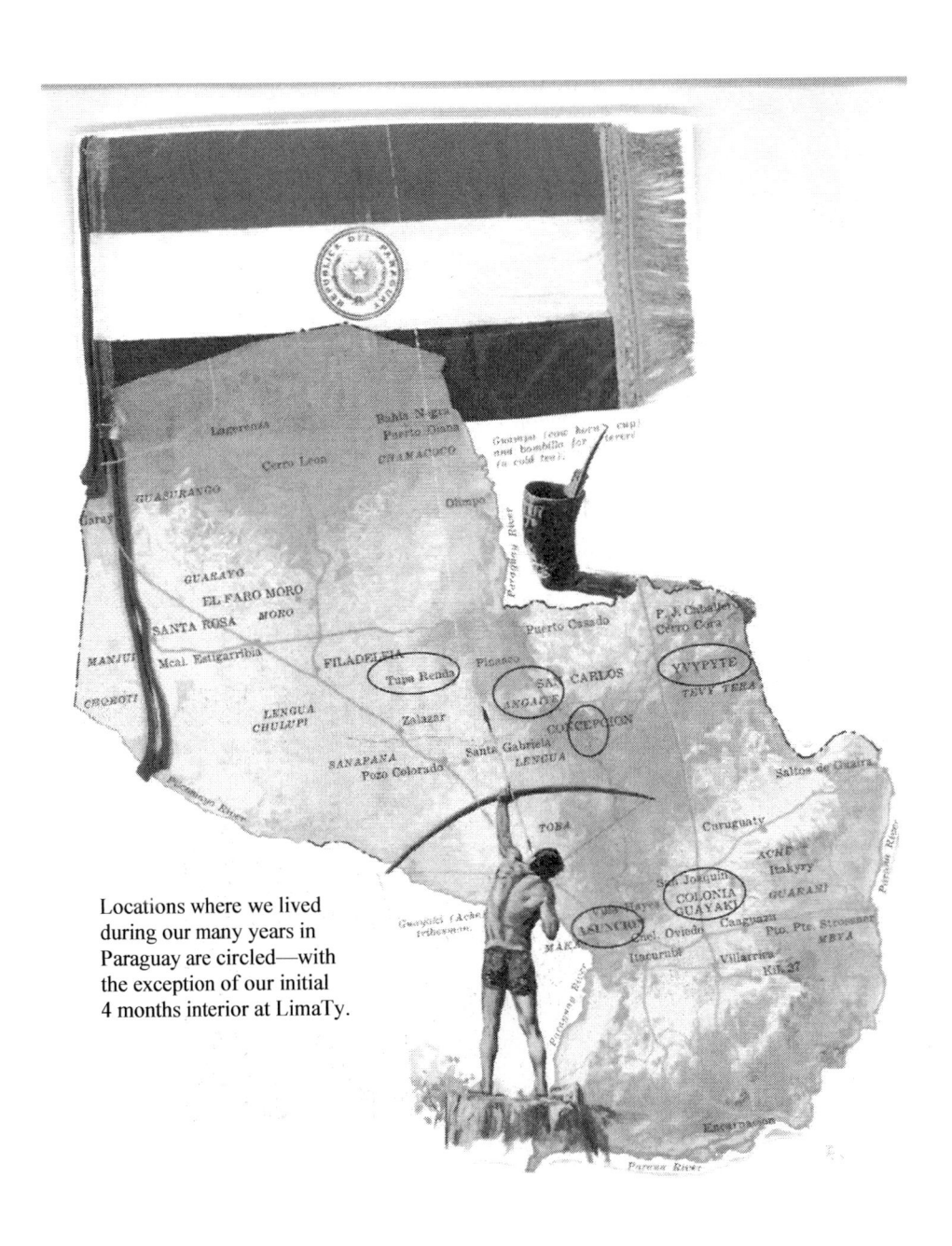

Locations where we lived during our many years in Paraguay are circled—with the exception of our initial 4 months interior at LimaTy.

Lessons Learned

Philippians 3:13-14: "...forgetting those things which are behind and reaching forth unto those things which are before, I press toward the mark ...high calling of God..."

LEARNED

I was once asked if I had any regrets concerning our ministry in Paraguay. I hardly knew how to answer that question at the time. I have no regrets for having gone to the mission field. But were there things I wish I had done differently? Undoubtedly, we all have wished we had done some things differently at one time or another. I'm going to answer this question by covering lessons learned that deal with family, co-workers and indigenous people with whom we lived and worked, as well as things I learned about myself.

Family:

Is there a parent who hasn't wished they were more experienced in their early years of parenthood? Hindsight can teach us a lot, but it doesn't change what was. When we have never been down that road before, we are more than likely going to make some mistakes. The important thing is whether we learn from our mistakes. What we experience as children growing up is often what we unconsciously repeat in our adulthood with our own children. No parent is perfect, but the children will pick up the prevailing attitude of the parents and know whether he or she is loved and accepted.

We already had teenagers before I recognized some things I was doing wrong. Thanks to some of our kids who were not afraid to say what they thought, I was able to correct some things. For example, I tended to be all work and no play. Work was something I was well acquainted with from childhood, being the oldest in a large family. It was hard for me to be doing *nothing*. And if I saw the kids doing nothing, my tendency was to give them more work. One day Dave said to me, "It doesn't pay to get our work done in a hurry; you just give more." He was right and I hadn't even realized it.

So what did I do about correcting it? I admitted he was right and apologized. I told the kids that when their assigned work was finished to not sit doing nothing in my sight, as it was hard for me to see them doing nothing when I had work to do; and I could always find them work to do. It sounds terrible to say they should be out of my sight in order to not be given more work, but that helped me break the habit of just giving them more work. I don't remember if they ever complained about being bored with nothing to do. It wasn't a safe thing to say to me.

Another thing that was difficult for me (which is embarrassing to admit) was how Fred sometimes chose to spend his leisure time in something I considered a waste of time. Although it initially bothered me to be working or studying college courses while he was doing something that didn't seem that productive, he was relaxing in the way that he enjoyed relaxing. What I was doing, I was also doing by choice—and just because I thought it a more profitable way to spend my time didn't mean he didn't have the right to how he chose to spend his. I didn't need to be his conscience. We each have a different way we choose to relax—and that's okay.

Co-workers and Indigenous People:

If I had a chance to do it over again, I would hope to be less critical or judgmental of fellow co-workers when in disagreement with them as to how they dealt with changes that affected the indigenous people. I found it hard when decisions were made that would not have been my choice, as I knew the change would be initially hard for the people to accept. I specifically felt that changes, however necessary they may be, should be explained as much in advance as possible so people could get used to the idea before the change took place. There should be good explanation as to *why* the change. Otherwise it was easy for the indigenous person to feel the change was being made only for the benefit and comfort of the missionary—not for the benefit of the people. This was especially evident when the phasing out of the work on the station was in view. I wish I had prayed more and spoken less—believing God could work in the hearts of all involved for a smoother transition. It would be helpful for missionaries to keep in mind from day one that they will one day be phasing out, and they should prepare themselves and the people accordingly for that day by not waiting too long to implement what they can as soon as possible—praying for the right timing of such, of course.

I would be slower to express an opinion on things that didn't matter that much, instead of having to put in *my two cents* worth when it wasn't going to change the situation anyway.

I know there were times I was too quick to speak when I felt there was a wrong, without first having spent sufficient time in prayer concerning the situation to see if God would take care of the situation without my help by convicting the other person or persons—be it a co-worker, family member, or an indigenous person. This was specifically true where indigenous believers were hearing false doctrine from elsewhere and were seemingly attracted to it. It may well need to be addressed—but with much prayer ahead of time so as not to alienate the individual. The indigenous person may have little understanding of why there are so many different beliefs among church denominations and religious organizations. Not that I didn't pray before addressing such a situation. I did. But sometimes I would have saved myself some regrets and hurts by waiting until I wasn't so emotional about a negative situation—and spending plenty of time in prayer to give God opportunity to prepare the other person's heart for what I felt I should share. Though I was quick to apologize and ask forgiveness if I offended another person, I often worried afterward whether or not the other person had really forgiven me—which is not healthy either. If an issue is that important, it's worth taking the time to be sure our own hearts are right and emotionally settled before addressing it with the other person.

There were times when, out of concern for sick individuals who were facing life-and-death issues, I may have spoken too harshly about the fact that medical instructions were not followed. Sometimes it was talking to an alcoholic husband and father who was the cause of his wife and children being malnourished to the point that the babies died. But until people really understand that they have a lot to do with their own health, by adopting necessary measures toward good health, it's useless to get upset at them. If they believe sickness is only caused by evil spirits, they will not feel responsible to follow the missionary's medical instructions when the medicine doesn't cure immediately. You might ask why they would even come to the missionary for medicine if they believe sickness is only caused by evil spirits. The witchdoctor is supposed to be capable of removing the evil spirit, and they are likely to try whatever recourse is available perchance one thing doesn't work—maybe the next thing will. They may think the missionary has the power to do the miraculous, in which case the cure should be immediate. Those situations call for lots of prayer too.

Just like we have reasons for why we do what we do, other people are the same, regardless of their ethnic background. I remember wondering why the Ache people were so indifferent toward building toilets (and using them), even if lumber was provided, until I learned they believed that evil spirits could enter them when they went to toilet. It's understandable with that belief that they didn't want to take the risk of returning routinely to the same place to toilet. Until that belief changes (probably only through acceptance of the gospel), they are going to continue believing what they believe, no matter what anyone says. And if a big issue is made of it—trying to convince them otherwise—they will just learn to cover up what they believe. Much prayer is again needed in having the wisdom to know how to respond to these situations.

If I felt another individual had something against me, for whatever reason, I would also go to speak to that person to try to find out what I had done or for what reason the person appeared to be uncomfortable with me. One thing I learned long before I ever went to the mission field is that I don't answer for anyone but myself. I am responsible for my part in any conflict, no matter how small I may feel my part is. If the other person refuses to recognize their fault in a conflict, then it must be left in God's capable hands.

I have found in such a case that my praying faithfully for such a person changes my feelings toward that individual—whether the other person changes or not. We often need to give the other person the benefit of the doubt (where sin is not involved), realizing everyone usually does what he or she feels is right at the time.

And what about changes in myself?

I would hope to be less rigid, not such a perfectionist that I wore myself out always trying to do more than is expected of most people—be it work I was doing for a coworker, for the indigenous people, or just pushing myself beyond normal limits to finish a project because another project was waiting for me.

Because I tended to be a high-energy person, I set a precedent of doing whatever was asked of me *right now*, if possible—as I never knew when I would have more time later. I felt under pressure if I had something in the back of my mind that needed done, so I attempted to fulfill others' requests as quickly as possible. This caused them to believe it was easy for me. Trying to keep that pace was often hard on my health. It was hard for me to let some things go that probably could have waited; no matter how difficult or time-consuming a project might have been, I tried to keep everything else in the home in order and organized at the same time. As I got older, that was harder to do. I had a hard time recognizing or admitting my limits. It was hard for me to learn to slow down—even though I was no longer young.

Interestingly enough, I never expected other people to put themselves under that kind of pressure and could counsel them (what I should have counseled myself) if they allowed themselves to get under pressure unnecessarily. Work was one thing I was comfortable doing; that's what I had known all my life. I had never learned to "play" and I was not comfortable doing so. I didn't have anything against others playing games, I just didn't enjoy it myself. I always had a list of goals I was trying to accomplish—which seemed more than I could ever get done if I took time out to do "nothing." I did take time for others who came to visit, but I wasn't much for sitting around talking about nothing for long periods of time. It frankly was an underdeveloped area of my life.

It was hard for me to say "no" when asked to do something, even if I knew it was going to put me under pressure to do it. The first time I actually had to say "no" to teaching preschoolers at NTBI when living there in the '80s, I went home and cried. Though it was very hard for me to say "no," especially to the person who asked me, I knew I had all I could handle at the time, and I was having physical difficulties besides. I learned something there while observing another person who couldn't say "no"—feeling it was insubordination to say "no" to leadership. I'm not speaking of not being submissive to leadership, but rather recognizing one's limitations and freely stating them in a gracious manner to the leadership so they understand.

The person I'm speaking of did a fantastic job at what he was there to do, but the day came when the leadership (maybe short on staff?) asked him to take on another big responsibility on top of what he already had. He felt he couldn't physically or emotionally handle more than he already had, so he decided to resign. When I found out he was leaving, I felt awful, as I knew how valuable he was to the department he was working in, and I said, "Why don't you just tell them you can't handle more?" Surely that would be better than losing this individual. But he felt it would be considered insubordination and left—which to me was sad. That opened my eyes somewhat to the fact that, even when we can't do everything we may be asked to do, it's okay to admit our limits and at least continue working in the areas at which we are proficient and can still function. It puts an unnecessary strain on others if we decide to just quit because we can't meet everyone's expectations. We will never be able to meet *everyone's* expectations.

I accepted a lot of "last-minute" work people wanted done, thinking the only option I had was to say I couldn't do it or be pressured into doing it immediately. What would have been better was to let individuals know that I was glad to do their work for them, but they had to give me some advance notice—not handing it in tonight, wanting it early the next morning. The indigenous teachers were especially bad about doing that—leading to many late nights for me. In that they weren't people who had ever learned how to plan ahead, it was difficult for them to do so. They had no idea how time-consuming it was or how much work was involved, as they only saw the finished product. Once a precedent has been set, it's difficult to change it. It's best to not let that happen from the beginning, if possible, outside of an emergency. And most things are not emergencies. Though they may seem *urgent* to the individual, are they really that important? Sometimes we get so bogged down with the *urgent*, that we don't get to the *more important*.

We certainly need the wisdom of God to know how He would have us to function. To ruin our health unnecessarily—even if we're doing it with a servant's heart—may cut our ministry shorter than God intended. And how much of our unwillingness to admit our limits is just our pride? I never wanted others to see me when I wasn't feeling well, or to know when I was having a difficult time. That is nothing but pride which God hates. May the Lord help us to care more about what HE thinks than to worry about what others think—when in truth they may not be thinking anything anyway.

Working closely with a missionary team in an isolated situation brings a lot more stress than living in the city where you may not know your town co-worker's every move. At least we found that to be so. How many people in this country know their neighbor's income, know how they spend their money, know what goes on in their house, know how they discipline their children (or don't discipline them), and so on? Do you know how your neighbors spend their leisure time? Who cares, right?

Well, living on an isolated mission station is very different. Frankly, it's much better to have those co-workers than to be out there all by yourself. You need the fellowship, whether you think you do or not. But not all personalities automatically "click" without a good bit of working at the relationship. It's not like being in a city or even a church, where you choose your friends. You learn to work with those with whom God has placed you. HE knows what kind of co-workers you need. While that co-worker may not be perfect, neither are you nor I.

A business friend told me years ago, "You learn most from those who disagree with you—not those *you* disagree with, but those who disagree with *you*." He was a smart man.

It's possible to wonder, how did that person ever make it out of "boot camp" and onto the mission field? We must keep in mind that we are all people *in progress*. We are all likely at different stages in that progress. May we love each other and encourage one another's growth in our walk with the Lord, as we all desire to live a Christ-like example before the people we have gone to reach for the Lord. God loves that co-worker you may be having difficulty with as much as He loves you. He has purpose in your working alongside each other. Trust that He knows what He is doing. I remember once saying to our field director our very first term on the field, "You know how hard it is to get along with___." He was very wise. He said, "No, I don't; you will go back there and make it work." At that time in my mind, I was certain he knew that person could be difficult, but if he did, he wasn't going to let me know it—or even give me an inch to excuse my feelings. I am so grateful he did that, because we did learn to work in that situation and to appreciate the very people we initially thought were difficult people to work with.

Many times when there are difficult personnel relationships, people are moved to another location where it is thought they might be a better fit. I'm not saying that is *never* the right answer, but in our case I'm grateful we weren't given that opportunity. There is no perfect place to serve, and there are no perfect people. Changing locations just means different problems to face and learn to deal with.

CULTURAL ADAPTATION OR FRUSTRATION

"Time-oriented" foreigners trying to live and work in an "event-oriented" society can be very frustrating if one doesn't learn to adapt. The reverse is also true. Surprisingly, the same people who are "event-oriented" and take their time arriving at a scheduled event may not be as patient when it is their turn to wait for *you* to respond to *them*.

When the indigenous school held special celebrations for Mother's Day or end-of-the-year events, nothing ever started at the hour stated. It could be as much as an hour or two later, with people just sitting around waiting until all the parents arrived. The only time people would show up early at special holiday events was when food was being served.

And if you get upset at the pastor or special speaker running overtime on Sunday morning at your church, you wouldn't want to attend an Indian church, where they may normally have as many as three preachers and sing until they're sung out.

Relationship-oriented vs. Work-oriented

Relationships are of utmost importance in an event-oriented society. In our American society today people hardly have time for one another. Not only do many people not know or talk to their next-door neighbors, but many families are scattered throughout the United States and the extended family may not even keep good contact, although it's an easy thing to do in this country with telephones, internet, and so on. The people with whom we worked in Paraguay cared very much about their relatives. When elderly parents died, it was considered a great loss—no matter how old the adult children were—as they were now going to miss having the wisdom and input of their elders. Age was respected in their culture. They liked to have as many of their relatives as possible living close by. When they were separated because of some having to go elsewhere to look for work, it was hard on them.

My white hair was an advantage in Paraguay, whereas it is a definite disadvantage in this country. Here the emphasis is youth and beauty, whereas there, it was age, experience, and wisdom. On the mission field, the younger people with whom we worked, as well as all the missionary kids, were very conversant and treated us as equals; we found it to be very different returning to the United States—another adjustment to make.

Included in the relationship issue with the Angaites—if they came to make a request and they felt you were too busy or not in the right frame of mind to grant their request, they would not say what they wanted. They would wait for another day when they thought your "stomach was sitting well"—in other words, until your spirit was such you were apt to listen with rapt attention and grant their request.

Another thing we found with the Angaite in relationships was that *anger* was considered the worst of sins. It was unforgivable that a missionary lose his temper for any reason; it may take a long time, if ever, to gain back the respect lost. They respected people who could keep their cool in a disagreement. Paraguayans may hate you behind your back, but they will generally be polite to your face. Americans often appear to them to be rude for tending to be so upfront and outspoken.

We are definitely called to Servant hood! May be found as faithful servants to the ONE who calls us to serve HIM.

Paraguay

50th Anniversary

On September 27, 2008, we celebrated our fiftieth anniversary at Grace Community Church in Ramona, California, all planned by our kids and their spouses, the grandkids helping as well. Dora made a flight from Waukesha, Wisconsin, to be here for that day. Her son Dan (in the Marines at the time) was able to be here as well. We missed Jim and the other three boys but were grateful Dora and Dan could be here. Everyone else was present, and they all worked together to make it a wonderful celebration.

They cooked and served Mexican food to at least seventy-five to eighty people. Steve had all our slides and pictures scanned digitally and put on a loop to show our work in Paraguay up on the church screen as people sat visiting. They showed our wedding pictures of fifty years ago, also.

Dean and Margaret Lattin (one of our former pilots and his wife, now retired from Paraguay) were present, making the day extra special as well.

Steve Thomason (nephew by marriage) drew a caricature picture of us; the kids enlarged it and placed it in the foyer of the church, where people signed in.

Our kids all shared, letting us know they appreciated us; Steve asked us to pray for all of the family, and then asked our pastor, Paul Nelson, and his wife Cathy to pray for us. It was a wonderful way to celebrate our 50th.

Made in the USA
San Bernardino, CA
23 March 2017